Ralph Steadman

Other books by Ralph Steadman

STILL LIFE WITH RASPBERRY
AMERICA
SIGMUND FREUD
A LEG IN THE WIND
I, LEONARDO
THE CURSE OF LONO (with Hunter S. Thompson)

illustrated by Ralph Steadman

LOVE AND MARRIAGE
WHERE LOVE LIES DEEPEST
ALICE IN WONDERLAND
ALICE THROUGH THE LOOKING GLASS
FEAR AND LOATHING IN LAS VEGAS
THE HUNTING OF THE SNARK
THE POOR MOUTH
CHERRYWOOD CANNON
EMERGENCY MOUSE
QUASIMODO MOUSE
THE DEVIL IN TEXAS

Between the Eyes

JONATHAN CAPE
THIRTY BEDFORD SQUARE LONDON

Publishers in a Best-selling Hat. by Ralph STEADman Jan 1984.

ACKNOWLEDGMENTS

A special acknowledgment again to Ian Craig who, whilst faced with an infernal blizzard of drawings, notes, no sleep, confusion and homelessness, calmed it all into place like an inspired Messiah, then disappeared silently one day into a mountain of rejects – and has not been seen since. At least he is no longer homeless and we leave things out for him.

Verite cum multum absentia.

First published 1984
Copyright © 1984 by Ralph Steadman
Jonathan Cape Ltd, 30 Bedford Square, London WC1B 3EL

British Library Cataloguing in Publication Data

Steadman, Ralph
Between the eyes.
1. English wit and humour, pictorial
I. Title
741.5′942   NC1479

ISBN 0-224-02988-6
ISBN 0-224-02280-6 Pbk

Printed in Italy by
New Interlitho, SpA, Milan

To my Teacher Leslie Richardson

Early Fears

Baggy Morgan's Adam's apple was combobulating furiously by this time and each pair of eyes in the workshop was following its every move – listening to it even, as it gurgled up and down to the accompaniment of a high-pitched Welsh tremble.

Baggy Morgan had very little flesh and every bone movement was dramatically visible. He hid his bones in tweedy-green suits which were as generous as he was emaciated – hence the name Baggy. But after five years of humiliating instruction and knuckle-rapping with the leading edge of a 12-inch ruler, you knew how to make a joint and how to 'screeoo' a 'screeoo' and how to 'gleeoo' a joint with 'gleeoo'. For a concentrated five minutes of any lesson, one of us in the workshop became an object of public ridicule, and all the other boys, for only boys did woodwork, bathed in the glow of not being the 'muggins'.

'And whar else are yeeoo holdin', boy?'

'A hammer, sir.'

'Gather round, boys, we've got a muggins eeyah!' It was Baggy Morgan, woodwork master at Abergele Grammar School, talking. The year was 1948. 'Whar are yeeuw, boy?'

'A muggins, sir.'

'A muggins, boy, and look at 'im, boys, and look at that chiss-el. What is it, boy?'

'A chiss-el, Mr Morgan.'

'Yes, boy, a chiss-el – and whar are yeeuw tryin' a'do with it?'

'I don't know, sir.'

'Well kill yourself, that's what, boy. Look at it – right at your stomach it's pointing – right at your stomach. One slip and – ! And whar is it you're tryin' to make, eh boy?'

'A joint, sir.'

'A joint! A joint!! Gather round, boys – this muggins ses 'ee's tryin' to make a joint, with the wrong end of a chiss-el too. Well we can all make jokes can't we. Look at that joint, boys – look at it. Well? What's wrong with it?'

'Sir, it doesn't – '

'Right Edwards, he didn't bother to check the size of the mortise against the tenon before he cut it and on the *right* side of the line, you muggins – the *out*side. The outside on the mortise, the inside on the tenon. You can always take more wood off but, and this is important, boys, YOU CAN'T PUT THE WOOD BACK ON AGAIN!'

The truth was so obvious when Mr Morgan pointed it out. A fact of life, inviolable, the stuff of reason.

Ralph STEADman

1937.

1939.

1939

me at NOWT   me at 3   me with Sister

1945

Me with Tishy and Alponse

me + Aeroplane 1950

Pensarn, Abergele   *1981.*   A 2112

me + Keith   Chris Aston

me, Ray + Trevor

Me at RAF. Roch
~~Me at MEAT?~~
The height of
a heady
career in RADAR
The crew of an
obsolete early
warning system
the end of WALES
Futility was RI
Not a single ear
warning proved an
effectiveness.

RAF 'H' Flight - Hut 254   Sunday 16 Oct. 1954

8

'Exactly, boy, a hammer. Where's your wooden mallet? Think of my chiss-el handles – yeeoo'll split 'em, that's what yeeoo'll do!'

Despite his fondness for the sport of 'catching a muggins at it' he was a kindly soul outside the woodwork class and the scrawniest of cartoon characters by any standards. All good experience in the rough and tumble of school life. Nothing savage or brutal but just enough to drive the boys round behind the bicycle shed for a quick smoke and a giggle, and that would be an end to the matter were it not for the morbid shadow that hung over the little red brick grammar school in Abergele, North Wales . . . When I first arrived as a green scholarship boy, the only piece of scholarship I can lay claim to, the school occupants nestled in the generous palm of a benevolent and understanding headmaster who at that very time was nearing retiring age, and maybe if he'd stayed throughout my schooldays I would not be blessed and cursed as I am with the unsocial habit of depicting my fellow man as a threatening mutation. Instead this gentle person retired in a cloud of genuine affection and a more sinister mood stalked the corridors.

Morning assembly became a public hanging place where children were taught to enjoy the sight of a schoolmate less holy than themselves suffering their downfall in public. It's too much for any child, the parading on stage of the one who has been caught, the holding up at arm's length of the offending material - a dirty poem perhaps, or a rude story of some kind – and every one of us has read it, enjoyed it, but we are innocent. *We* are the assembly. But the poor wretch of a girl is not alone on the stage. She is flanked on one side by

Me and Mirabelle

my Family - my sister Barbara is seated between the ducks

9

A certain amount of 'hush-hush' hypocritical murmurs seep out to protect the carrier from this reaction but once we all know who the carrier is the temptation is to distance yourself from the source by mouthing verbal reprisals couched in pious sympathies for the poor wretch who has been detected and particularly for the guilty parents.

The irony is that nits only attach themselves to clean hair and that suggests either bad luck or that all the other children are unclean.

The sensible and most humane course of action would be to allow *all* the children to get them, and the teachers too of course, as quickly as possible, and eradicate the social stratifying that a local outbreak causes, so that nobody is a victim.

The real nit is our interminable class structure. It is not the medical danger or the unpleasantness that gives us the shock, but the realisation that those bent on social climbing will be found out and suffer a setback in their own community. Social climbing is our national sport but the trick is not to get caught doing it. There's nothing like a nit to make people think they know where you are from.

I lay awake at nights in the top floor attic bedroom of a three-storey block of council flats listening to the wind beating the roof and lifting

a row of perfect prefects in gymslips or green blazers and grey flannel trousers and on the other by upright ageing spinsters, stiff with frustration and safe behind pock-marked faces and turkey-flesh necks. And the men of course – disappointed thinkers fighting to keep their ends up and keep down any natural sense that this is a travesty and an inhuman ritual, but maybe they've forgotten anyway and everything seems quite normal, or they are simply afraid. It isn't even cowardice. Authority prevails and quashes any doubt before it even emerges. The boss is enjoying himself and displaying an unswerving belief that the law is fear and pain is duty and shame is necessary to grind the edge off the spirit and blunt it into submission. This is humiliation of a darker kind. The real world, perhaps. We are learning the rules the hard way and the only lesson of it all is that you must not get caught.

A tremor of fearful anticipation ran through the school like a ferret with rabies – 'The nit nurse is coming today!'

The social stigma attached to an actual 'find' in a child's hair is a trauma for the parents, a serious setback for the child, an open wound and source of tormenting amusement for the other children to play on and even a reason for cruel reproach if another child has caught it from the official 'victim' – as though it were the child's fault.

I REMEMBER GRANNIE...

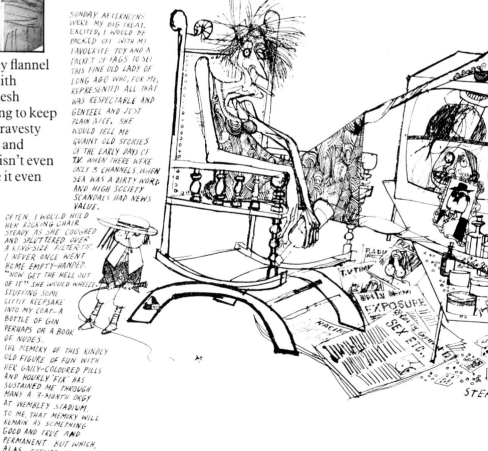

SUNDAY AFTERNOONS WERE MY BIG TREAT. EXCITED, I WOULD BE PACKED OFF WITH MY FAVOURITE TOY AND A PACKET OF FAGS TO SEE THIS FINE OLD LADY OF LONG AGO WHO, FOR ME, REPRESENTED ALL THAT WAS RESPECTABLE AND GENTEEL AND JUST PLAIN NICE. SHE WOULD TELL ME QUAINT OLD STORIES OF THE EARLY DAYS OF T.V. WHEN THERE WERE ONLY 3 CHANNELS, WHEN SEX WAS A DIRTY WORD AND HIGH SOCIETY SCANDALS HAD NEWS VALUE.

OFTEN, I WOULD HOLD HER ROCKING CHAIR STEADY AS SHE COUGHED AND SPLUTTERED OVER A KING-SIZE FILTER-TIP. I NEVER ONCE WENT HOME EMPTY-HANDED. "NOW GET THE HELL OUT OF IT" SHE WOULD WHEEZE, STUFFING SOME LITTLE KEEPSAKE INTO MY COAT — A BOTTLE OF GIN PERHAPS OR A BOOK OF NUDES. THE MEMORY OF THIS KINDLY OLD FIGURE OF FUN WITH HER GAILY-COLOURED PILLS AND HOURLY 'FIX' HAS SUSTAINED ME THROUGH MANY A 3-MONTH ORGY AT WEMBLEY STADIUM. TO ME, THAT MEMORY WILL REMAIN AS SOMETHING GOOD AND TRUE AND PERMANENT BUT WHICH, ALAS, OUTSIDE MY MIND, IS NO MORE (TEARS).

the skylight and on some nights even the sound of the waves which seemed to carry remarkably well from the beach considering it was 400 yards away across a railway track that led to Rhyl and the outside world. On some nights I couldn't even hear the waves at all. But I was safe in that attic bedroom. I used to shut out all the things that troubled me at school. I had no need to confront the algebra teacher or the English mistress. I was locked in a world of my own, designing and constructing model aeroplanes.

Any one of us could have loved English as a child. Most of us didn't. There are always the odd few, but perhaps it was swotting they liked. To discover the joy in language we must first be made aware of its possibilities. A young mind must be gently led, shown how humour emerges. Something a child can relate to, something funny – and then the expression of tragedy perhaps, in a smaller portion, not a massive tome to wade through. Not merely a technical device or a bunch of questions for an exam but an explanation of how the words can shape and express our emotions and how all great writers invented their own solutions.

My schooldays became a burden. I lived in mortal fear of authority and did my best to be good but with an ulterior motive: to avoid confrontation and personal involvement. My homework was tackled and finished the moment I got home so that it would not hang over my own time like the sword of Damocles, and then I would throw myself into my own pursuits – the model building, photography, clockwork trains and chemistry.

I was now bottom of the class and therefore could set my own low standards.

Schoolmates looked to me to provide them with a yardstick, someone much lower than they were so that by comparison they looked pretty good. I was popular because of it. A community needs someone like that, Some poor bastard to chain to the oars.

You could even convince yourself that you were different and therefore mad, and your only friend was your own reflection. The ones who considered themselves mad or 'a bit of a card' never really impressed me because they worked at it and it struck me as too unnatural to be real.

Effervescent joke tellers were everywhere hiding their own shyness, or lack of originality maybe, behind a 'new' joke and telling it to as many people as possible before anybody else, to establish authorship and live off the glow of laughter until the next time.

What need provokes my drawing apart from the serious one of making money? If that were the only reason I would have tried to please people, so maybe I'm a crusader of some kind hell bent on changing the world for good or ill. A pompous thing to say, but you need people like me. I couldn't keep thinking up jokes to fit little drawings for evermore. I thought to myself – Christ – I can't imagine spending my whole life doing this, there must be something else. There must be another way to unite the art of cartoon and the drawings I was doing at life-classes and art school generally, so that each helped the other. For I found that the more I learned to draw, the more difficult it became simply to draw a funny face with a big nose that was the same face I drew yesterday and the day before. Something else began to creep in which initially was more of a

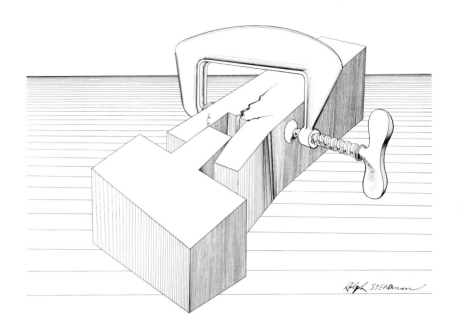

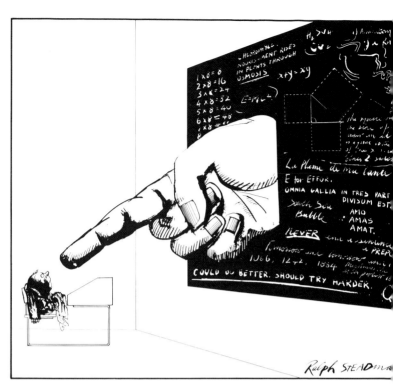

12

hindrance than a help. It was a need to express character but it lent itself more to pure illustration than to cartooning and during that transition I still had a living to earn and in effect it was a bit like changing jobs without actually having one.

I did a drawing called Plastic People, sent it to *Punch*, who rejected it, so I dropped it in to a new magazine called *Private Eye*. It was 1961 and the magazine had just started. I got a letter from Richard Ingrams saying, 'Here's a fiver, more power to your elbow.'

An act of divine intervention as far as I am concerned. *Private Eye* gave me a platform of great scope and freedom and even indulged my odder whims. (I had to say this, otherwise they would have had a go at me.) Our association gave me confidence and I tasted reaction from an otherwise indifferent world.

I tried some more. The real stimulus, however, was discovering George Grosz and John Heartfield, and *The Age of Gold* by Luis Buñuel. Grosz and Heartfield were part of the Dada movement, itself committed to a kind of political art, the art of rejection of all values. A declaration that any society that can promote wars such as the Great War must be corrupt, therefore society's values must be corrupt. Nothing could be taken seriously. They held their first exhibition in a Zurich toilet and offered axes at the door to the public in case they became so incensed that they felt the desperate need to smash what they were looking at and thus make their own comment. The challenge was too intimidating, the movement too self-deprecating and thus its life was short.

But that was by design, to create themselves and obliterate

themselves before their revolutionary ideas found favour with the bourgeois collectors who would elevate them in the same way that they elevated those artists who were part of the system they despised. They endeavoured to possess the ultimate control over their own destiny. If they wished to commit suicide as a movement, that was their right. Timeless art to them was anathema. Their art belonged to them and the last thing they wanted was to thrust it upon the next generation.

They were grasping for purity in their originality – 'the shorter the life the less corruptible'. The ideas the movement left behind spilled over into the latter half of the twentieth century through the spirit engendered by Marcel Duchamp, its unofficial leader, which still inspires artists today. Ironically we are still the victims of cultural tyranny just as we are victims of the bomb. Once thought of and created, it cannot be obliterated.

My first cartoon.

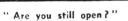

"Are you still open?"

edited by
JULIAN PHIPPS

STEADman

STEADman

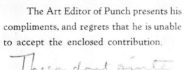

PUNCH OFFICE,
10 BOUVERIE STREET,
LONDON, E.C. 4

The Art Editor of Punch presents his
compliments, and regrets that he is unable
to accept the enclosed contribution.

These don't quite ring bells. I'm passing the "Bureau" inspite of the boxing boots, but I would stress the inadvisability of straining for effect

My first self-portrait, aged fifteen.

"But this is the way we did plan it."

"C'mon luv—it's your favourite."

WELL CAN I GET YOU SOMETHING?

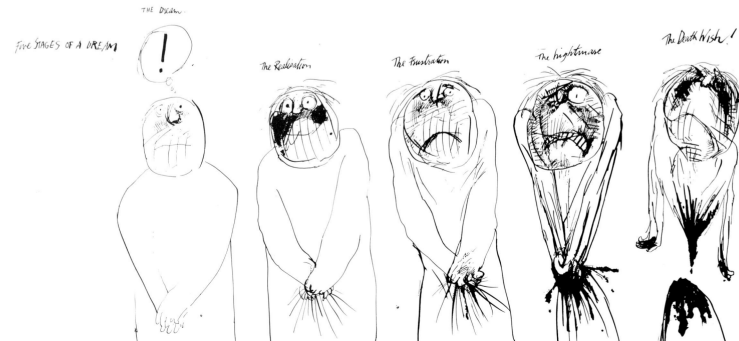

My signature alone must suggest something to somebody. Why stop printing my surname in capital letters half way through, then pause, thicken the 'D' and half-heartedly add the 'man'? I used to be Stead – at least that is what I called myself. It was my mother who wondered whether I was ashamed of my full name. I hadn't given it a thought until then. I was merely looking for an identity with a short sharp name that everyone would remember.

So even then I was seeking fame if not fortune. It was nothing personal against my family name or my family. They are very dear and reasonable people. I love them all, even my sister. God knows, I have reason enough to hate my sister – who hasn't? Don't think I haven't considered murder at times and don't think she hasn't either. My sister looks like Maggie Thatcher – not just superficially, but deep down too. She sounds like her and just like Maggie she brandishes the frightful habit of being right at all times, like someone wielding a bread-knife.

Even as a young man I had huge ears. They didn't grow huge, they were huge from birth. It was my head that was smaller to start with so that from behind I resembled a butterfly with mumps.

But I had a lovely mop of curly hair and my mother cultivated it like an orchid grower, but to her credit she never entered me in a baby show for she is a woman of such sensitive caring and I take after her. They are my father's ears.

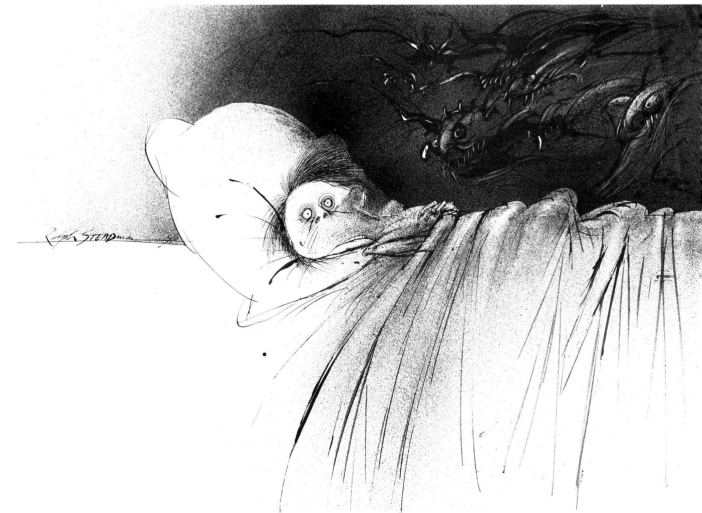

My drawing grouch

The whole art school system is bereft of discipline and direction. It is wallowing in a sea of helpless acquiescence as it watches year upon year of successive students pass through its hands, knowing that it has not bestowed upon them so much as the skill to draw a circle around a plant pot.

Drawing tended to go out of fashion after artists like Picasso had gone as far as they could with representational art. 'Basic design' was

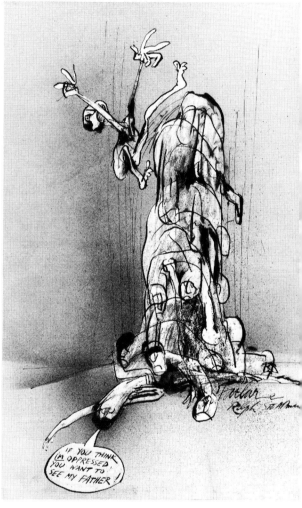

the new exciting teaching method, sweeping away 'academic drawing' as old-fashioned, associated with empire loyalists and camiknickers. I believed in it myself for a time, but my pressing need was to earn a living (it was my background, you see). My approach was utility, banal and immediate – and still is. So be it. If we have to live in a world where being useful in society is being serious and law-abiding, then we can play the game providing we realise that a game is exactly what it is. We are not going to be lawyers, accountants or doctors. We took art instead of Latin.

Negative attitudes to art begin in school. Art is not taken seriously because it has no apparent rules. We are declaring ourselves non-rational beings, i.e. people who intuitively act upon impulses without rhyme or reason.

We are only necessary when we as artists can be seen to be exploiting an intangible flair in a way that brings gainful employment within the system. Muck-spreading propaganda will do, if you like, as long as it is paid and promotes the attitudes of the day. But if we get beyond that point we are on our own. Dangerous and, in society's eyes, useless. This puts art schools in the invidious position of promoting potential rebels, alien creatures and doubtful neighbours. In this way art schools are on dangerous ground, for whilst trying to awaken exciting creative urges in their students, they must also attempt to teach some basic skills which will at least serve the future of those blessed only with an eager but mediocre talent.

For a student, creativity should be the last lesson. If it's there, let it be but for the moment, learn – look – absorb – study. The situation of teachers is more complex. Time has gone by. They may have compromised. They probably have financial commitments. They may compare themselves to the students, creating an inhibition that students need never know. Exercising their own creativity through students is a huge temptation, for an apparent glitter in end-of-year shows may appear to display a teacher's effectiveness. But I believe it is only superficial. A discipline achieved early on should become as automatic as breathing or talking. And the discipline of drawing is the finest. A savage two or three years is imperative. No creativity. Drawing forces you to look and an artist needs to do that more than anything short of thinking. But drawing will stimulate that too. Then give yourself a break and waste a year in total anarchy. Vent that precious creativity you have nurtured for so long and find out what you might have to offer – bearing in mind that the unsuspecting world does not give a rat's flash.

Beer Street

21

Is it not possible for art schools to re-establish themselves as protectors of values? In an attempt to convince a sceptical world that they have modified their act to serve a material society, they have denied the harder course; that course which reminds us that we need spiritual nourishment as well. But since the subject of art is kept at arm's length in our educational structure I can appreciate the dilemma. Purity of intention should be a guiding maxim. The moment we decide to enter an art school we should feel that we have taken our own Hippocratic oath to see it through. We are doctors of the spirit and if an operation is necessary – then it must be performed. Here we stand, here is the situation: we need to convince others, to embrace them, to incorporate *all* people in a world of imagination as a natural part of our everyday life.

Discipline and a thorough work programme are necessary right through that tender period where nothing is really known of one's ability. I suspect that when they arrive students hope to be guided; to be told what to do and to hell with the idea of free expression, at least in the early years. It's no bloody use to them then. They might as well spend their time trying to fart accurately through a puncture.

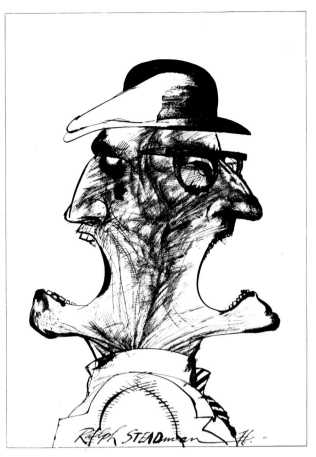

CUT ALONG DOTTED LINE

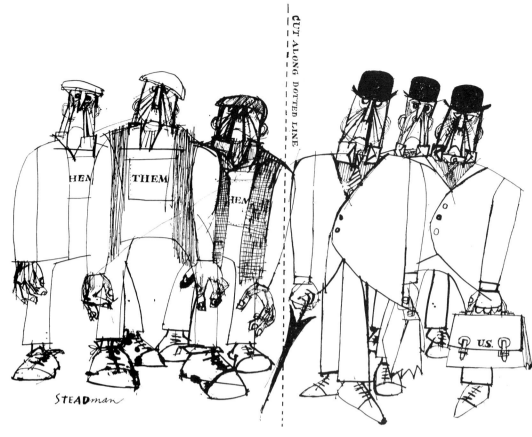

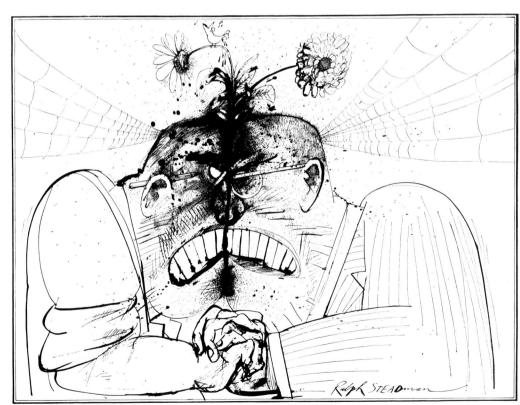

Mona Heath

STEADman

Gardening Hint No. 19

Neighbours are a gardener's worst enemy, no matter how nice they are.

I personally don't mind the ones I've got holding a rock concert in their back garden, particularly with such a great lineup: Butt Frenelli on lead guitar, Gaston Harrison on drums, Morry Manzarek on bass and Elvin Sandlin on electronic triangle and clavichord. And of course my plants love it.

I OKed it when they assembled scaffolding over my garden to make seating for 100. I didn't mind the coke and hot dog stand on my begonias. I waived the heavy use of my outdoor toilet for snorting and god knows what. I laughed uncontrollably at the frenzy amongst my hydrangea bushes.

I gathered momentum at the sight of rock-crazed goadies churning my lawn into a mudbath and I finally snapped when these good folk lost their self-respect and stole – yes, stole – my beautiful rich ruby Sunrise tomatoes, which I was about to gather in myself after months of careful nurturing. Then they peed on the naked stalks. If only these people knew how silly they looked!

Tomatoes are fairly easy to grow and even

sier with these fantastic new Gro-Bags
available everywhere. It's late to start growing
em now, unless you have a heated, bullet-
roof glasshouse, but a few tips for next
ring:

The Gro-Bag makers rightly claim you can
ow four plants in one bag. I say, grow two
d double the quality.

When planting, sink a small plant pot so
at the lowest roots can get the water.
omarite is OK for feeding young plants, but
hen fruit appears, the finest fertiliser is made
om a mixture of poodle blood and horse shit.
ut since the rock concert next door I'm going
experiment with my neighbour's basset
und.

Tie your plants well, supporting each truss,
nd stop off the top of a plant (cut the top
oot) when four trusses have formed.

The tomato season may be prolonged by
cking late fruits when they are just beginning
turn colour and storing them wrapped in soft
aper in a cupboard at 45°-50°F.

The rock season may be prolonged by getting
e hell out of my area. Next time: Growing
r the lean years in an old Ford.

Go get soiled.

Human proportions: According to Leonardo da Vinci "The span
of a man's outstretched arms is equal to his height" So far
Harold Wilson is all correct! But consider further:
From the chin to the starting of the hair is a tenth of the figure: From the
junction of the palm of the hand as far as the tip of
the middle finger a tenth part:

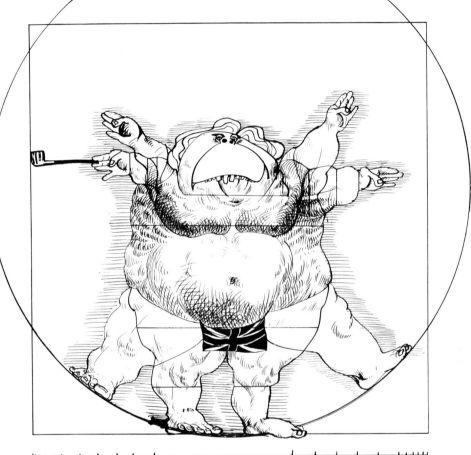

From the chin to the top of the head an eighth part.
And from the pit of the stomach to the top of the chest is a sixth part: And
from the fork of the ribs as far as the top of the head a fourth part: And from
the chin to the nostrils is a third part of the face: And the same from the
nostrils to the eyebrows, and from the eyebrows to the starting of the hair:
And the foot is a sixth part, and the forearm to the elbow a fourth part. The
breadth across the shoulders a fourth part: There is as great a distance
between the commencement of the one ear and that of the other as there is from
the space between the eyebrows to the chin: The size of the mouth in a well-
proportioned face is equal to the distance between the parting of the lips and the
bottom of the chin — and so on. And this applies to a sound man at his
zenith which Harold Wilson presumably is! I say Harold Wilson is
all **WRONG**!!

Ralph STEADman
1967

Not being an active political animal, I have never been an attender of meetings either locally or deeper into the fray at national level.

However, I am nothing if not an avid TV watcher and bitchin' from an armchair, I'm sure, is far more vehement and widespread when there is no one to scream back at you and have you forcibly evicted. People like their comforts. What better way, then, than to sit at home with a beer in one hand and a fag in the other and tell some two-faced politician just where to get off?

And do it eloquently too.

A law-abiding citizen can sleep easy in a bed after a bout like that and know that all is well and the cause is won.

There must be nothing more frustrating than going to an important

The Black Dwarf

ESTABLISHED 1817   VOLUME 14   NO. 15   FORTNIGHTLY 1/6d.

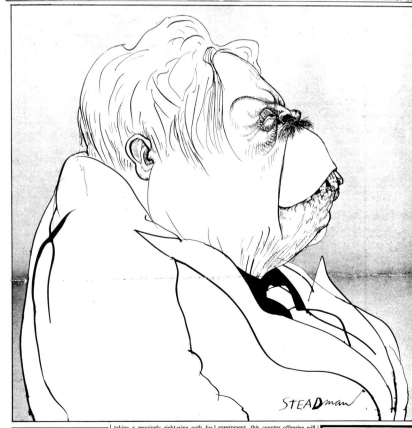

taking a genuinely right-wing path for that would destroy the party within a matter of weeks. Thus unable to go | government, this counter offensive will move from the level of demands to the level of actions. The working class will | IKE

DWARF

meeting with a brilliantly modulated question, only to be shouted down or not even given a chance to ask it.

Years ago, from the comfort of a bedsit in east London I made mincemeat of Harold Wilson and he damn well deserved it too!

These were the 1960s of course, when everything was possible and things were going to change. We weren't going to be fobbed off with platitudes any longer. We wanted answers and we seemed to be getting them, until a few of the smarter politicians like Harold and Ted Heath learned a newer language and turned us into foreigners again in a foreign land.

So far we have never recovered from that singular experience and even now we all suffer from an indefinable despondency which will only disappear completely when the passing of time itself puts paid

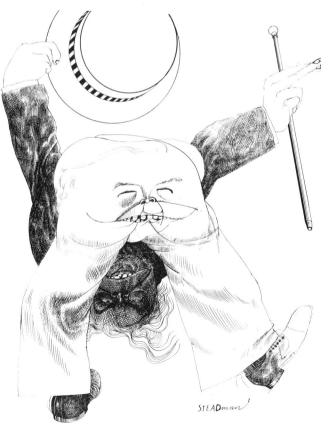

27

for ever to the crimes we mistook for social change. The 'White Heat of Technology' will eventually make slaves of us all and nothing then will matter anyway. We can't have it both ways.

'When the gods seek to destroy governments they first tempt them into illiberality. For the misuse of power arising from the arrogance of office first manifests itself in straining, where Ministers are entrusted with quasi-judicial functions.'

Harold Wilson, April 20, 1964

December 15 1973

Rolling Stone:

So what if this is 1973, ten years after the first Kennedy assassination evoked some of the most shockingly callous racism imaginable; nigger-hating, or rather baiting, is still apparent in this aboveboard/underground leftist magazine in Steadman's sketches of 'Dallas '73'. It seems that after all of the consciousness raising of the 60's, when such demeaning racial slurs became hushed private affairs, stereotyping is now in vogue again. Steadman's gross portrayal of a black woman at the Elks' Convention, and his assertion that there were Cadillacs in front of poor southern ghetto houses is incredibly cruel and pointless. Even in satire, any black artist would have treated his subject much more humanely, with respect and love even, and still have expressed what I think Steadman is trying to say – that black economic and social progress does not make for a change in values. But so what? Are you disillusioned white boy? Can you now retreat back into despising black people with new justification?

M.M.

January 14 1974

Dear M.M.

I'm sorry you feel the way you do about my Dallas '73 piece and even sorrier because *Rolling Stone* only printed one-third of the material I did there. The things I wrote and drew worked in sequence and explained a much more humane and understanding point of view than ever came out in that castrated version you saw but now the damage is done and *you* can retreat back into despising white people with new justification which was the phrase you threw at me and now I throw it back and a slanging match begins and that makes me so fucking sad. And I can't blame *Rolling Stone* for what happened either, as it is just one of those editorial things that happen sometimes in the process of assembling a magazine and I have to shrug my shoulders and let it go or have one good blast and forget it – which I hope is what you have done.

I know how lucky I am to be able to express my views publicly; it gets a lot out of my system and on it hangs a responsibility and I try and remember that, and sometimes I get bawled out like now and that's OK – except when I'm misunderstood. Between you and me I think we both speak the same language.

Ralph Steadman

28

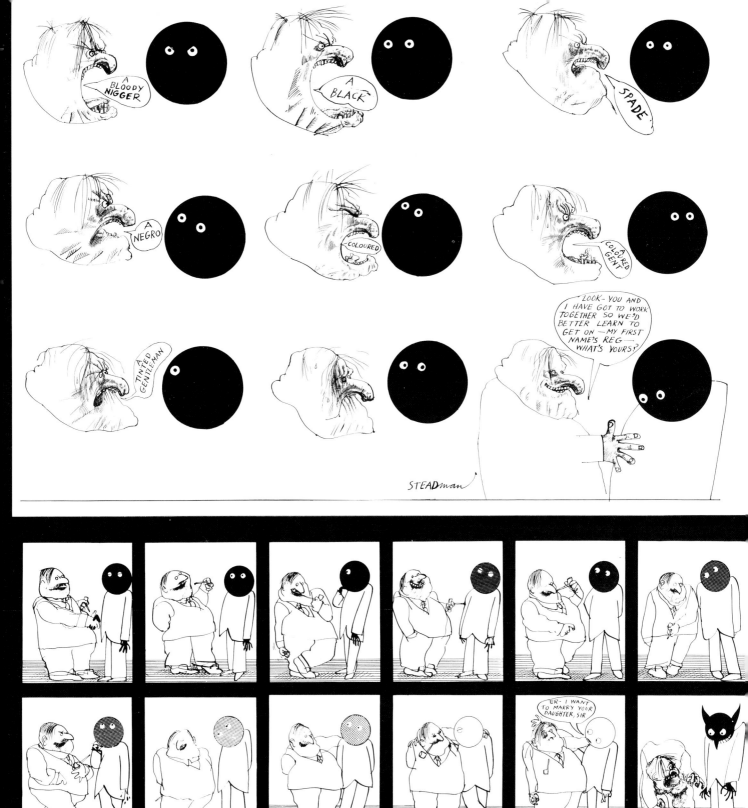

I realised at once, of course, that plants are like children. When you talk to them they grow. If they are noisy, you say, 'Shut it, you snivelling little banshee!' And if they continue, you just put the boot in, as Dr Spock now reassures us is OK.

Gardening Hint No. 8
Ever since Professor Marcel Dupont of Verdun University and Directeur du Bureau d'Affaires Horticulturales (Ypres branch) stated in public that the growth of plants and flowers is greatly improved by talking to them, I have been of the same opinion. But what he did not say was what you talk to them about. After six years of experiment in controlled conditions I think I have a few pointers to offer readers.

As plants rarely make a noise it was difficult. I first approached an Aralia Sieboldi which, as you know, is the poor man's Monstera Deliciosa, and tried to tell it about my sex problems. Within a week its leaves fell off. Now that, I admit, could simply have been overwatering, but I carried out the same experiment on a particularly virulent Russian vine, and, sure enough, within a month it had turned in on itself and started to grow into tight coils.

It was obvious to me that plants don't like problems. They have enough of their own. So I just chatted pleasantly about the weather, and spring-was-just-around-the-corner sort of things, and sure enough my Hoya Carnosa threw out two new trailing shoots inside of two weeks. I also discovered that a Cryptanthus Bivittatus stops in its tracks with intellectual talk; and politics is out, and economics and divorce and particularly didactic chat on how to bring about social change during an energy crisis.

Basically, plants and flowers are simple souls who like the over-the-garden-wall approach: 'What are you having for supper?' A touch of

gossip about neighbours' love affairs. Flattery. That sort of thing. Don't underestimate your plants' intelligence, though! A fatal mistake. Don't get cocky and fool around, but tell the odd joke by all means. And they quite like being talked to by desperately lonely people, provided they keep it jolly.

Next time – what to sing to your vegetables.

Gardening Bathtub Death

The other night I was sitting in the tub reading The Guide to Gardening by Ralph Steadman when the radio fell in and electrocuted me. What can this mean?

Timothy Spann, California

'Just a stone's throw from here,' my agent said, 'the tall silver building with the diagonal roof like some kind of steel cutting tool. On 53rd and Lexington. Not far. The First National Citibank. You'll see the name outside. Take the elevator to the 20th floor, show your ID, sign on the dotted line, take your money and away you go.'

I was inside the building on the ground floor within three minutes, panting a bit, but nothing a jet-lagged forty-year-old who rolls his own couldn't control. Escalators fed a shopping precinct under the building and the elevator shafts dominated the centre of a shining lobby floor beneath my navy blue non-slip deck shoes. The elevator signs indicated 15–31 in large green-lit modern numerals all along the left side between the two blocks of elevator shafts. I didn't look at the other side. No need. By my reckoning 20 had to be in there somewhere.

I pressed a large white button the size of a saucer and didn't have to wait. Ding, went the elevator bell. The doors opened immediately, zip-a-doo went I. I sprang inside an empty elevator, swivelled on my navy blue deck shoes and in mid-swivel jabbed neatly at a number 20 on a red button in a vertical line of red buttons. I slumped against the back of the lift with my hands on my hips, caught my breath and waited. The doors stayed open. I jabbed it neatly again. There was a hesitant twitch, then the doors closed smoothly. I was alone in a box 8 x 8 x 4 feet. I felt the swish of wind and acknowledged the stomach-turning sensation as the high-speed elevator shot upwards. I idly scrutinised the control panel and noticed a vertical line of green buttons too.

My attention was caught suddenly by the first level number to light up in a large round glass panel on the left.

15 – 17 – hmmmmm – then 19 – I got ready to nip out nimbly and collect. 21 – 23 – 25! – what the? 27! – then – deceleration – slow – stop – over a kind of rise – and then descent. Down, down – 25 – 23 – 21 – ah! now – 19! Christ! No! 17 – 15 – blank – deceleration – slow – stop – then whoosh, up again – 15 – 17 – 19 – 21 – 23 – 25 – 27 – at top speed too – Holy Shit! What? I kept jabbing the red 20 – deceleration – slow – stop – then down again – 25 – 23 – my heart quickened; my stomach had long gone – 21 – 19 – 17 – oh god! I could feel the panic rise and seize my nerve ends – 15 – blank, deceleration – slow – stop – then up I went again – 15 – 17 – I jabbed frantically at the red 20 – 19 – 21 – oh please god, why? I was trembling now as I reached in my pocket for a bottle of valium in a vain attempt to ward off a dark wet blanket of claustrophobic terror coming down over my head – 23 – 25 – 27 – and – down again.

It must have been sheer reflex action that guided my eye to the black (why black?) emergency button on the same control panel and I pressed it. A bell sounded like a burglar alarm and immediately a voice crackled out of microphone slots on the very same panel.

'Somethin' wrong?'

'I pressed the emergency bell,' I said. 'The lift! It's going up and down and I can't get out. Get me out quick, it won't stop.'

'Hang on, buddy,' then a pause. 'Which level do you want?'

'Any fuckin' level, just stop the lift. I'm feeling horrible! Please!!'

I was going up again – 17 – 19 – the voice crackled again.

'Have you tried the "door open" button?'

'Wha – ?' My voice was failing me now. 'Wha – where?'

'On the control panel. Calm down, buddy. We'll get you out. Press the button that says "door open". Bottom left. Below emergency.'

There it was, right there and I went for it like a wild pig shot from behind. The elevator was on the turn again at this point: 27 – blank – slow – stop – 25 lit up. Pause . . . Oh no! Noooooo!

'Still there?' the voice crackled again.

'Eeeeaaooo – argherr,' I whimpered, then – 'I think it's stopped.'

'Press "door open" again, keep calm! Everything's under control!'

I pressed it again and oh heaven! It opened and I fell out. No, I think I leapt out sprawling on the carpeted floor of some corporation reception area in full view of a beautiful black blonde beyond a pair of smart glass doors.

I heard the voice crackle again from inside the elevator.

'Did it work?' said the voice.

At this point I must have lost my sense of reason or perhaps I was just overwhelmed with gratitude and relief, for I scrambled up and stumbled back inside the elevator to address the microphone.

'Y-yes th-thanks,' I stuttered. 'I-I'm okay, th-thanks. I'm fine.'

Then it happened. Albeit in slow motion, but it happened: the doors closed again and I was still inside. Yes! I pressed 'door open' again. Nothing happened this time except that the lift began to descend – 23 – 21 – 19 – 17 – 15 – blank – ooooooh god!!! Help meeeeee!! – blank – eeee blank – eee – blank – bleeeeeee – e – e – e – and a kind of a numb horror followed me down.

That's it! Of course! It's a fight between god and the devil for my soul. Up – down – up – down – up – down:

'He's mine!'

'No he's mine!'

'Leave him to me!'

'Keep your thieving hands off him, you filthy bugger! He's our sort. He's no use to you!'

'He wants me, I heard him call my name. He cried out for me!'

'You're fullashit, god – he's on his way down!'

'You thievin' devil, Lucifer! You get all the good ones . . .'

The slowing sensation brought me round and I was standing stiff as a garden gnome against the back of the lift. The doors opened and fourteen New York bodies crowned by fourteen New York heads all preoccupied with their own hopes and fears for the future poured into the lift.

The doors closed again and fourteen different fingers jabbed fourteen different times.

I had to say something, anything, to somebody or anybody. I know people walk the streets of New York in blind terror though their faces are fixed in masks of sublime composure. Husbands who have just cut their wives into ninety-nine pieces and left them for dead in the waste disposal come out like guardian angels to help old ladies across the street. Child molesters buy hot dogs, window-shop and quietly sit in bars. Blackmailers smell flowers and feed the birds in Central Park and lone assassins figure out privately whose death would create the greatest shock news value as they thoughtfully scratch their groin inside their pocket with the butt of a gun. Those are personal nightmares people can handle, but mine could no longer be

33

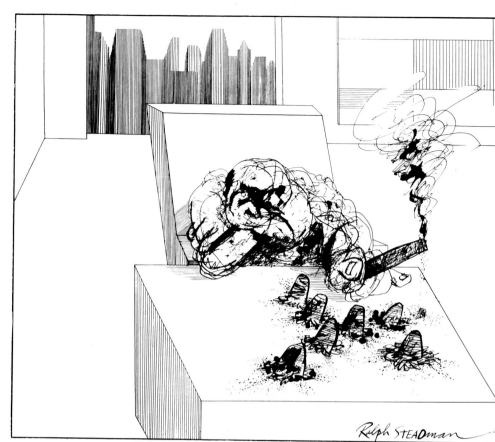

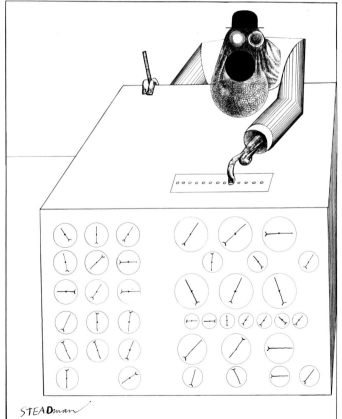

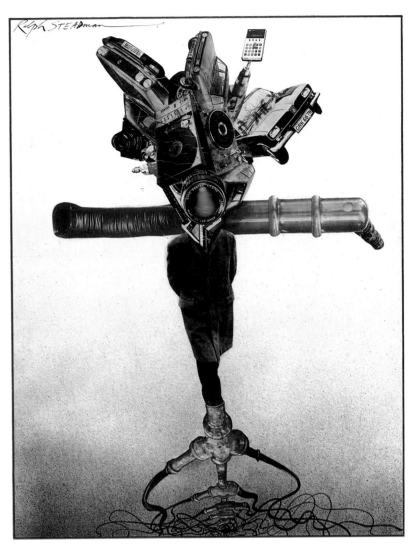

contained. Where was the voice, the friendly microphone crackle I had acknowledged only moments ago? Was it only a computer, or did it live and feel and say I love you?

People act differently in lifts, partly because they are temporarily confined but mainly because they are unnaturally restricted in their movements by other bodies in close contact. If fifteen people stood like this in an open space anywhere else, in this building in fact, they could get arrested – or at least one of them could, for indecent behaviour. So people withdraw inside themselves, look upwards and keep their hands clasped in front.

An old lady, wearing two overcoats and wellington boots and carrying two canvas bags that I knew contained everything she had in the world, was crushed up against me. I spoke.

'I – I'm afraid I have just had a frightening experience,' I said limply and not directly at her. Her eyes looked up at me through a face of beaten pewter and I had to look down at her.

In a loud voice she said, 'I never talk to strange people, I only observe. Somerset Maugham *never* talked to strange people either and look what happened to him!'

'What happened to him?' said a droll voice from somewhere else.

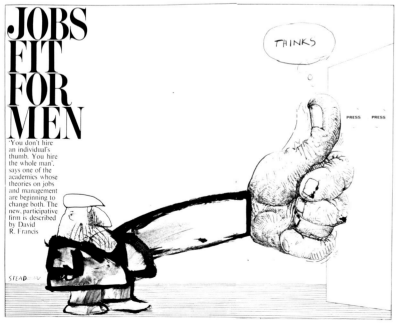

'It's none of your business,' said the beaten old lady, 'but he always wrote it down.'

The lift stopped at 15 and instinctively I tried to move.

'I have to get out,' I said.

'I always write things down,' said the old lady.

Someone harumphed, someone cleared his throat and the elevator stopped at 17. This time, three got out and two got in. I couldn't move. I was feeling faint and the trembling had become noticeable. People tried not to look at me – 19 – 21 – the elevator stopped. People got out. I was rooted to the spot. The doors closed.

'Where are the missing floors?'

People turned and looked directly at me in a strange way for the first time. Nobody spoke, not even the old lady.

'I'm looking for my floor,' I said. 'I want to get out, but I can't find my floor. It's disappeared, has anybody seen my floor?'

'Steady there, mac, what floor? Whaddya talkin' about?'

The elevator stopped. A sign flashed. 'Car loading.' I read it. Twice.

'What's that, what car? Where? Why can't I get out? Why has the lift stopped? Get your hands off me! I'm a British citizen. I know my rights. Leave me alone!'

'Calm down, buddy. What's the problem?'

'He's mad. You can tell – he's mad. Look at his eyes.'

'No, *you're* mad, you're *all* mad! Get out! Get out of my lift! It's my lift! Get out! Out!! Out!!! Everyone has a right to a roof over their heads. This is mine! I found it first. It's mine.'

I must have been waving my arms about as well, for thirteen people no longer able to communicate with me formed a tight caucus hard against the doors which opened at the 25th level and spewed them out in all directions like shots from a 12-bore leaving me alone again, a spent cartridge. Spent, but not without my reason. Oh no! There are moments in everyone's life when one acts from a sense of self-preservation. One wild leap took me well beyond the closing doors which half a second later would have shut on me for ever.

For a moment, I was standing open-legged and arms akimbo like Harrison Ford in *Star Wars*, facing the beautiful black blonde through the smart glass doors. I shrugged and walked forward. I had a grip on myself by now.

'Could you tell me where the stairs are, please?'

Not taking her eyes off me for an instant, she replied, 'Stairs? There are no stairs, sir. Except in an emergency. You'll have to take the elevator.'

I gripped the side of the desk to keep my voice steady.

'Then – then can I – can I use your phone?'

She pushed it forward without looking down. I dialled my agent.

'Hello, Nat? It's me, Ralph. Can you come and collect me? I'm on the 25th floor of the First National Citibank on 53rd and Lexington. I think I'm stuck.'

The Onion Seller

Onions! An enormous number of them, really, hanging like too many balls on a Christmas tree. Hanging on a bike standing against the wall outside the Prince Albert in the Albert Bridge Road. There was a kind of British Railways tea bar excitement lying heavily on the place as I walked in.

At the bar sat the onion seller – he couldn't have been anything else. A woman with a dog was sitting in one corner, one or two other folk were dotted around like pieces left standing after a game of chess, and the barman leaned heavily on his left hand to relieve the fibrositis in his backside.

I ordered my usual, a Guinness, and sat down with my collected works of Lewis Carroll and a piece of paper to take notes and make brief sketches for my interpretation of *Alice through the Looking Glass*.

The barman was ordering two skeins or whatever of onions and as the onion seller moved towards the door, I impulsively placed my order for a string of the same.

The onion seller returned and placed the onions over a chair in front of me and continued into the back with the other order.

The bar door opened again and in walked a youth wearing a small blue beret. His faded turtle-neck sweater was two sizes too big for him and he carried a polythene bag with a few papers inside.

Walking straight over to me, he spoke. 'Are you the onion seller?'

'Er, no. He's through there,' I said lamely.

Hesitation, then, 'Mind if I sit down?'

'Please do.'

He feverishly produced a squashed packet of Players No. 6 and offered me one – I was smoking.

The onion seller returned. 'Are you the onion seller?' said the youth.

'Yes.'

'Do you ever go near Epsom?'

'Er no, I'm afraid not.'

'Pity. I'd like some of your onions but I can't carry them all that way – there's no point. Do you make a lot of money selling onions?'

'No, not really.'

'How much do you make?'

The atmosphere in the bar changed from one of convivial boredom to iced uncertainty in a split second and I found myself reading, 'What a number of

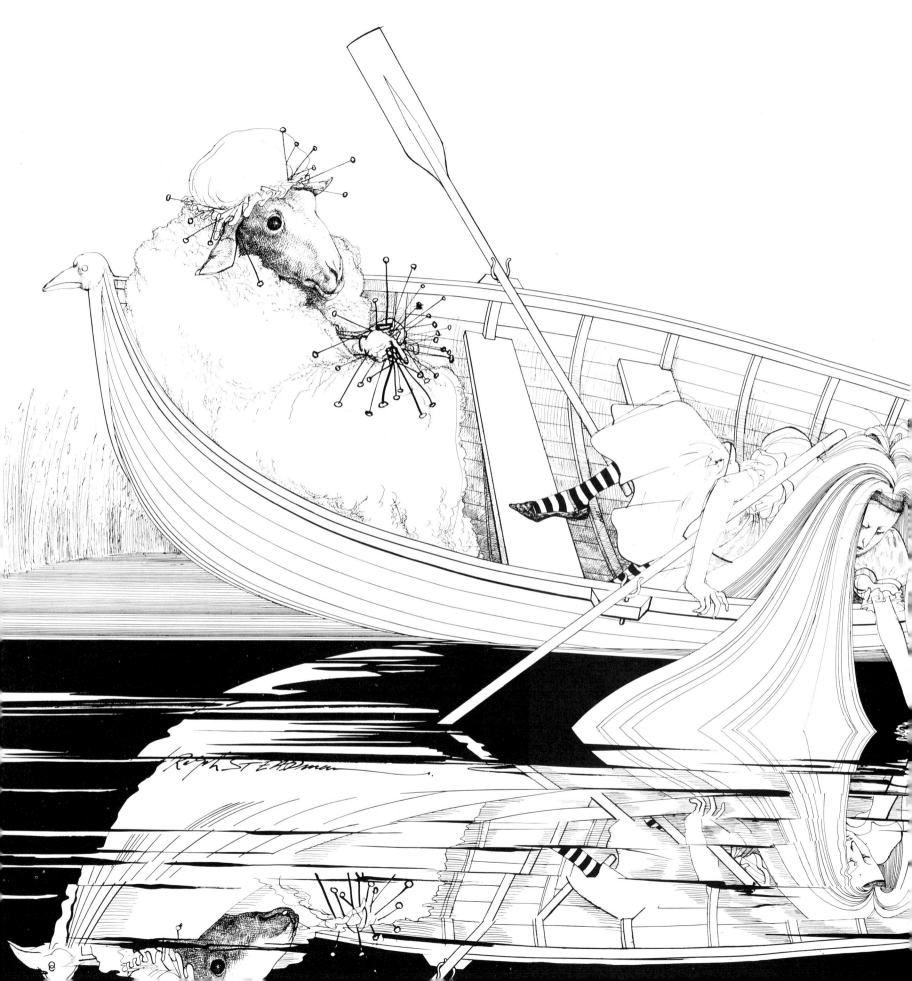

people there are in the carriage, thought Alice,' over and over again, trying to read on, but unable to. My mind was riveted by some fear I could not define. The youth was transmitting bad vibrations.

He turned to me and I tried to keep calm. I doodled on my notepaper.

'Are you an artist?'

'Well, a cartoonist.'

'Oh, that's interesting. Who do you draw for?'

'Oh, *Private Eye – The Times* – even the *Red Mole*,' I added hastily, as if to qualify myself to this person who certainly wasn't a *Times* reader, or a *P.E.* one if it came to that.

'I'm a writer,' he volunteered impulsively, poking his cigarette in the ashtray. His hands were shaking quite visibly. He too must have been very nervous.

'Oh, really,' I said. 'What do you write?'

'Well not much really at the moment. I'm writing for the Revolution. The Revolution is coming and make no mistake about it.'

The onion seller was looking at me with a sickly smile, in fact there were sickly smiles all over the bar – people in a strange situation look to others for some sort of reassurance. Nothing had really happened, but something had changed and this was puzzling. The fear of some unknown nothing was at work.

People's eyes suggested what they hoped was true – this man was a nut and must be treated gingerly until he could be safely guided out of the situation and preferably into the street.

'Do you know Tariq Ali?' I said, using the first name to come to mind.

'Well, he has his work to do and I have mine,' he said, trying to look

39

mysterious. 'That book you're reading. It's full of messages. The dialectic is the important thing. Chinese philosophy contains all the prophecies and Lewis Carroll used words mathematically to prophesy what is coming about. You've heard of *Winnie the Pooh*, haven't you?'

'Yes, it's become a rather middle class cult, hasn't it?' I replied.

'Precisely,' he said, 'precisely.'

'Can I have a glass of water?' The barman quietly filled a glass from the tap under the bar and brought it to the table. The bar went silent. No one was sure what to say next. The youth fumbled in his pocket and brought out something which looked like a transistor radio.

Unwinding the carrying cord wrapped around it he pulled out a small drawer in its side to reveal a dial rather like that on any other radio. Then quite deliberately he held it up to his ear and listened – everyone listened and watched. I tried hard to look at my book again but the words had become meaningless.

The barman broke the silence. 'That a wireless?' he asked.

'Yes, but it's not the kind you know – you can't get Radio 1 on here. This tells me all I want to know about the Revolution. Where to go, what to do, who to see.'

He closed it up again, wound the cord around it and placed it inside the beret on his head.

The barman was wearing a glazed face as he came from behind his bar and walked up to the table where the youth and I were sitting.

'Is he a friend of yours?' he asked me, trying to smile but finding it difficult.

'No,' I said, 'I never saw him before.'

'Oh dear, oh dear, oh dear,' he said, 'you can't do that.' And he took the glass of water from the table, and he whistled through his teeth, 'Oh dear no.' Embarrassment and a complete breakdown in controlled reaction brought out a few more 'Oh dears'.

'Well, I just did, didn't I?' said the youth, and getting up he walked to the door. 'I came here to meet an onion seller and an artist and I've done that – so I'll be off.' And he was.

41

Early STATES

It's pleasant enough to embark on a transatlantic flight without viewing it through an alcoholic haze. There seems no need or even much pleasure in such a course this evening. And besides, this is part of my new policy to play a cooler game in America.

'Welcome on board, ladies and gentlemen. This is the Pan Am 103 flight to New York.'

'You hope,' mutters a man next to me with a foreign accent. He has answered me once already when there was a certain amount of commotion in the seating arrangements and people were shuffling about trying to settle down and put their coats and hand luggage in the overhead racks.

'Sorry to be such a pain,' he said, after disturbing me for the third time.

'That's OK!' I said benignly. 'We're all happy now.'

'Oh, I am far from that,' he snapped.

'Oh!' I thought. I've got seven hours and twenty minutes sitting next to this one and he's reeking of Brut.

However, going on first impressions is always a mistake and the man proves to be an interesting companion and very intelligent computer boffin.

The flight generally is routine, the in-flight film *Flashdance*. Arriving in New York, customs is quick. It's my face. Honest, clear,

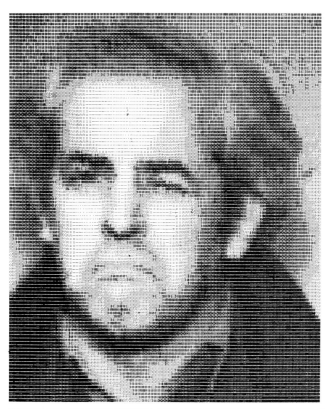

no pimples.

Getting a taxi, however, is a little difficult.

A crowd of touts offer their services. 'Wanna taxi?'

'Oh – yes.' I'm caught for a mo – can't take a look to see if there's a regular cab. There are crowds trying to get one too.

'Where d'ya wanna go?'

'The Salmagundi Club.'

'The where?'

'Salmagundi.'

'Never heard of it. Where is it?'

'47 Fifth Avenue.'

'On 47th Street?'

'No, number 47.'

'On number 47, downtown?'

'Hey Lou! Where's 47 downtown – near 8th or sommink.'

'Maybe on 9th or 10th.'

'Wait here – I'm getting other passengers.'

'What! Look, never mind,' I say, 'I'll get my own cab.'

'I am a cab, whaddya want, so there's a cab.'

The tout is organising other touts. Grabbing other unsuspecting passengers. Tired passengers. Unresisting.

I look over to the regular rank. A fat black official with a walkie-talkie in his belt is handing out tickets with numbers on. So that's it! Official tickets. A kind of queue-forming system.

I move forward to get my . . . bugger this man.

'Hey where you goin'? Got a ticket? You wanna ticket? What for? You gotta cab.'

'No, forget it.'

'Hey bud – 47. I'm taking you – relax.'

He is interrupted. All the touts are in confusion.

'I'll take him – you want him, OK, you take him – where – 47 – what – never heard of it – OK, OK, relax – he's yours – no you wan' him? Hey bud, where ya goin'?'

I am going to get a ticket whatever the wait. Patience is better than this confusion. I'll wait in line. I move purposefully forward and ask for a ticket. Number 40.

'12, no. 12.'

The big black man bawls out the next taxi – no. 12! God, I'll be ages. Never mind. The other is a rip-off and I don't feel like that – not at first.

'12, no. 13!!'

'14.' Oh, not too bad.

The tout tries again. 'You don't mind waiting? OK. OK – wait – I got a cab. I think somewhere around no. 33.'

Everyone in confusion. So I just get in one. Horns blaring. People lost, confused. Grab something, so I do. Out – marvellous. A cab of my own. Brooklyn cab driver. Talk of seat belts. All the way there. I ask a simple question, are they compulsory?

'Yeah, we gotta have 'em in de car but I never wear 'em. Maybe in some states.'

Arrive forty minutes later. Twenty dollars. I am relieved. Impressive high steps to old style, Pall Mall-type house. Twenty-five dollars with top. Leaves me on steps. There is a light in the hall.

Notice: watercolour classes, 6–10 on Fridays, etc. Notices. No sign of life. I try the door – locked. I knock. Look for bell. Knock again. Look for bell. Knock again. Scout through letterbox. Rattle door. Oh no, nothing, nobody coming. What! No one. Try again. No. No lights anywhere in rooms. Strange. Nothing . . . Bang!! bang!! bang!! Sod it! Now what. 11 o'clock at night. On the street. New York. Sod it. Why? What for? All for a lousy lecture. And I'm expected to give my first one at 10 am tomorrow.

I knock next door at a block of flats. Porter. He comes. I explain in

The New Anti-Hijack, Ultra-Safety Scaling Arrangements for Modern Air Travel.

44

as English a way as possible to allay fears of my being crazy. Get change. Phone box – on the street. Phone numbers in turn. Ansaphones. All of them. I declare myself. Ralph here. Help me! Be it on your own head then – you're out. I'm on a New York street late at night. Homeless.

Don Katz is last. He is out too, or asleep. People will be sorry.

Edward, Edward Booth Clibborn. He got me into this and he gave me a number in New York where he would be. A sleepy voice. 'Wha? – who – English, oh yes! . . . ah yes, get into a cab.'

Edward is sprawled on a divan when I arrive. He is stark naked, but covered half and half with a duvet. He is looking embarrassed. Half rises. Half hides himself. Pretends to rise. One leg off the divan.

'You got me into this, Edward – so here I am.'

'What happened?'

'Locked out.'

I spend a restless night in a short bunk bed, hastily fixed up by people who are pretty well still asleep.

Lecture goes well. Many calls. Organise the Salmagundi. It doesn't take bookings on Sundays.

'Oh, no one told me.'

Place is a musty old men's art club – where old artists go to die. Vintage Chelsea Arts Club atmosphere. Pictures on walls all up a central square staircase of past members. Old Colonial domiciled Englishmen. Old boys' network sort of place. Sons of the American revolution.

I am the only guest. At night it locks up at 11 pm. I think even the porter goes home. It's a fine building, but has seen better days. My room has a splendid old marble fireplace. Stuck awkwardly in a

corner, not quite fitting into an alcove, is a teachest-style wardrobe: cheap, grubbily painted in white undercoat. Bed's OK. But there's no money for renovation. That's obvious. One of those places where you know people must come and go but you never see them.

Sign in the hall of someone rearranging pictures. There's an impressive central skylight over the staircase.

In the lobby, a telex system like early Graham Bell. Chaotic pigeon-hole post boxes for members.

Where are the members?

Odd notes left for them – probably dead or gone away and become lapsed country members. The biggest drawback is no phone in the room. But it's like having your own huge New York house – all to yourself. A genuine brownstone.

Downstairs in the restaurant cellar cum snooker room, there is a declaration in old gothic writing: TO MEN THESE STEPS ARE SACROSANCT. ALL FEMALE POACHERS WILL BE SPANKED.

Well – I knew this was one of those places.

As I accustomed myself to the lifestyle over many visits, the feelings subsided but the desire to express them never left me.

The simple childlike way Americans manipulate their extreme philosophies inside their social structure is probably the right way. The first pioneers would not have survived as they did if they had thought too much. The country is too big to be understood by thinking. It is a physical country and requires muscle and native

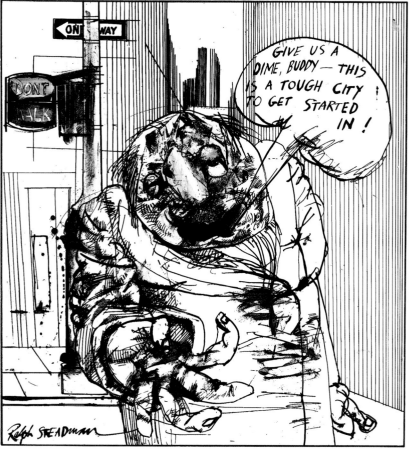

cunning to operate. Americans are afflicted with a kind of madness – but they are not insane.

Middle American Potwurst . . . sort of sausagelike form with bulges. Covered in dark cherry-red slimy white checkered nylon slick clothing that doesn't quite contain the contents . . . and white shoes

. . . you've got to wear white shoes.

It's bloody difficult for one as disgusted and uptight as me to become a tourist.

'Be a tourist!' I said. 'Go on – look gaga at everything. Relax. Enjoy the view. Make colour slides you can be justly proud of on those long winter evenings. Delight your friends back home with fun stories. Hire a car and get about. This is no time to relax!' I corrected my wife. 'You are with me to help seek out the bitter truth – *not* to enjoy yourself. *This* is an assignment.'

'Your car's out front, sir,' said the Hertz lady. I moved instinctively towards the mini-French Opel. 'No sir, that one's yours,' she said, pointing to a monstrous green Ford horror with a front and a back like aircraft hangars.

We gave an unusually friendly Texan a lift into town. He sat next to me with his baggage against the dashboard and his knees hard against his chest.

Santa Fe

By the time we reached Santa Fe I had got the hang of things.

Although we didn't realise it we had arrived right on the weekend of the 52nd Indian Festival.

Say no more. We'd see it all. The hotel was perfect. No air-conditioning. Just open windows and warm beer. Home from home!

What's going on?! North End Road, Fulham, London, SW6 was never like this.

Instead of vegetables, fruit and cheap plastic handbags there were Indians . . . Indians are despicably colourful. Overwhelming. Bless their blood red hearts.

'Keep a steady hand, lad – and a savage eye – it's not real. Cynical, boy – cynical. Steady as you go. This is 197–, not the landing of the Pilgrim Fathers.'

What the hell's the use of standing on top of a Navajo Bread Wagon and screaming 'You rotten, filthy, blind-greedy turquoise vultures!' when all around you 15,000 middle Americans whom you have just insulted with your constipated vocabulary bury their troublesome faces deep into another 1500 dollars worth of the luscious stuff and carry it off to God knows where whilst 500 willing state-controlled Indians egg them on with cries of 'That's for you, man – that's just for you!'

I mean, on those terms it's like pissing against the wind.

Sunday was a day out to meet the really real Indians – 60 miles north of Santa Fe on Route 285 to Taos Pueblo where the Adobe houses rise up five storeys in pure mud and straw.

Entrance fee – a dollar fifty. 'Oh! you wanna take pictures, sir? That'll be another 2 dollars – Is that a sketch book?'

'Er – yes.'

'You wanna sketch too?'

'Er – yes, of course.'

'That's another 5 dollars.'

'Oh, I – er – have my oil painting kit with me also.'

'You have? Another 25 dollars, sir.'

'Hi!' A beautiful little Indian girl sits down on the crossbar with me. 'What you doin'?'

'Oh, I'm sketching your beautiful houses. Do you live here?'

'Uh huh,' she replies.

'You've lived here all your life?'

'Uh huh.'

'Well, you probably take it for granted and wonder why all these people keep coming here just to —— .'

'You wanna take my picture?'

'Well,' I replied, delighted, 'I was actually going to ask you – I'd love to.'

'OK.' She moves away from me and adopts a pose like a totem pole.

'Beautiful.' Click! 'Thank you.' I resume my drawing. She comes and sits next to me again. 'You're very friendly.' I continue to draw trying to make conversation. She moves around me, looks over my page, fidgets and then braces herself.

'You ain't allowed to take pictures if you don't pay.'

'Oh, but I paid,' I said. '5 dollars to sketch, and 2 dollars to take pictures – even 25 dollars to oil paint.' I continue to draw uneasily.

'Well, you ain't paid *me*!'

'Oh, you, well, I thought you came with the price at the gate.'

'Nope! Children are extra. I'll take a quarter.'

Oh, for a paddle in that stream. Why not? Shoes off! Whoopee! Splash – Budweiser and all. Bliss!

Santa Fe Plaza

49

'Get your filthy sweating tourist feet out of that sacred water!!' An obvious Indian wearing a seersucker suit and two-tone shoes bears down on us waving an indoor TV aerial. Time to leave.

Raw Meat

Ideologies are the work of upstarts. They are essentially reactionary creeds which are designed to work like a violent laxative on a society or group of people whose bowels they wish to move or at least disturb. I prefer the term 'group of people' because that suggests a crowd of individuals with visible faults, real bowels and warm virtues, while 'society' suggests a heavy mass, with built-in solid bowels which are unmovable. Perhaps that is where upstarts go wrong. They mistake a group of people for a society and inevitably the group, made up of you and me, suffers bowel movements on a monstrous scale in aid of one person's ideology.

Here a few choice words regarding ideologies:

revolutionise, bowels, anus, damn, Monday, upstart, violent, brain, monstrous, creed, suffer, change, write creeds, tyrannise.

I fed these words to my computer, which replied thus:

To change people you must revolutionise with them. There are a number of ways to go about changing a person's bowels. Walk up to them on the street, grab them by the anus and yell 'Damn!!!! You

THE FATE OF THE UNKNOWN DISSENTER

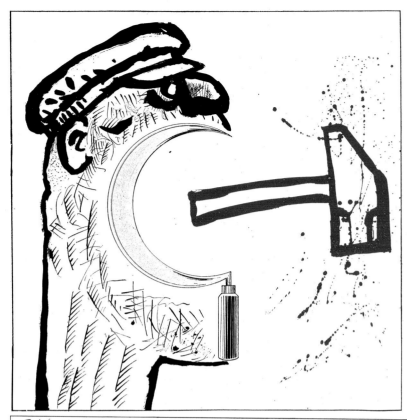

Monday upstart', or catch them asleep and whisper violent, violent, violent in their brain or set yourself up as a monstrous society and pretty soon people will start to suffer.

To work this alternative, though, you must either have a change you can change society with, or, do a write creeds or a tyrannise. But only if you aren't mistaken for a Monday upstart.

Get them by the balls and their hearts and minds will follow.

There is a kind of evil that has become OK. The term 'evil', sir, is relative. I don't quite recall, sir . . . no one wants to perjure themselves.

. . . twisting slowly, slowly in the wind . . .

Propaganda relies on the lowest mental response for the highest physical effect.

I'm even beginning to doubt my own lies.

If we were in Germany in the old days, you'd be a lampshade and I'd be smiling.

Enough of the Marxes of this world and anyone else with bright ideas to put everything right or left. Enough of the Boondoggle spawned in untutored minds only to emerge as witless cant. Great brains in all fields have filled our libraries and our art galleries with the most beautiful thoughts and still the world is rife with hunger, poverty, pain and misunderstanding. It's time to cast off all the dogma and clever quotes mouthed with such conviction. It's time to stop and ask the question, who am I? It's time to put on your coat and pull your hat well down and go out to face the blizzard head on. It's time to follow me.

You've got nothing to lose but your social benefits.

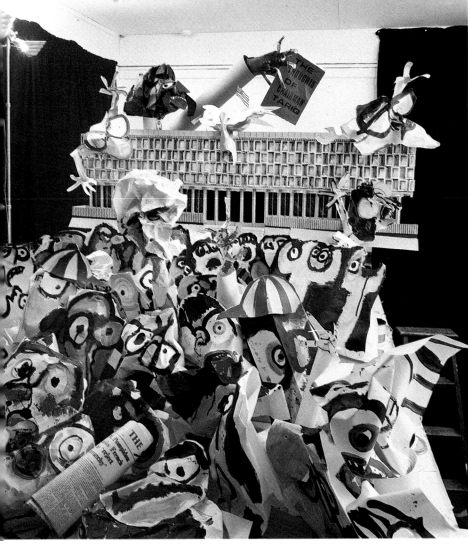

Some years ago, whilst I was still living in London, the following message was handed to me across the doorstep. I don't know if I deserved it, but I do remember the lady who handed it to me. I had inadvertently coughed down her neck whilst walking behind her up Oxford Street. Pure coincidence? Maybe. She accused me of filth at the time.

It seems she has got a lot off her chest here and she may be right. She obviously wishes her views to be known. Therefore I publish the text as a public document, without prejudice. I am sorry it has taken so long. It may be too late.

At least it may redress the balance for coughing down her neck in Oxford Street. It was not intentional.

The use of an automated range of thermal anti-matter weapons, working on an unpublicised principle, that are comparable to something that has evidently been with us in prototype for centuries, that allow the singling out of individual people and animals, and parts of them, with atomic precision, or that can settle a drought or a burning heat, or a freeze, on a whole area (for example, the atmospheric inversions in New York, Los Angeles, San Francisco, Paris and Rome in recent years, the unseasonably warm weather experienced in Britain last spring, and the drought and famine that has been afflicting up to 30 million people in five countries south of the Sahara for seven years) finds the Public without defence or information, and the Authorities mute and paralysed. People should be clearly made to understand that the greater part of all illness and disease is artificial and is imposed mechanically as a means of tyrannical control, oppression, and murder for profit. Conditions for which this statement certainly holds good include: 'viral' attacks, miscarriages, arthritis, multiple and disseminated sclerosis, poliomyelitis, still births, 'cot baby' deaths, thrush, croup, rheumatic conditions, lumbago, slipped discs, arteriosclerosis, strokes, hernias, abscesses, boils, acne, tumours, polyps, warts, cysts, piles, flatulence, eczema, herpes, erysipelas, psoriasis, chilblains, scarlet fever, mumps, measles, chicken-pox, cowpox, diphtheria, corns, bunions, swollen joints, diabetes, ulcers, varicose veins, kidney disease, dropsy, elephantiasis, 'dropped wombs', floating kidneys, coronary thrombosis, HEART defects or malfunctioning, nervous and mental symptoms, manic depressive states and so-called mental illness, amnesia, hypertension, hypomania, lassitude, neurasthenia, subnormality, involuntary sleep, narcolepsy, encephalitis lethargica, fainting, comas, catalepsy, hypnotic trances, levitation (weightlessness), post-hypnotic

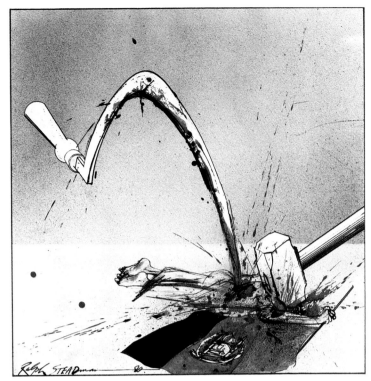

suggestion, insomnia, migraine, meningitis, phobias, manias, allergies, cravings, yens (impulse buying, kleptomania), etc. Constipation, influenza, cholera, typhoid, dysentery, D. and V., diseases of the urinary and digestive tract and prostate gland, fractures, gout, septicaemia, gangrene, osteomyelitis, bronchitis, asthma, stunted growth, weediness, weeny-bopper state (now extended to the entire British Public, and the further development of which can at any time be paraplegia through 'muscular dystrophy'), gigantism, fits, hypothermia, chills, bilious attacks, car and seasickness, alopecia, baldness, premature ageing, arrested or premature development (physical or mental – puberty on a sliding scale), dyslexia, aphasia, eye diseases, defective sight needing spectacles, cataracts, glaucoma, blindness, detached retinas, deafness (to sell hearing aids), alcoholism, DTs, fallen arches, hammer toes, cramps, reinforced LSD trips, drug addiction, sciatica, shingles, bedsores, speech defects, hysteria and hysterical signs, 'psychosomatic' effects, tooth decay, silicosis, autism, hirsutism, cystic fibrosis, sleepwalking, haemophilia, pneumoconiosis, jamming firearms, rearing horses, opening rear doors of DC-10's, and receding gums. Any part of a person can be eroded or shrunken, or blown up, and one can be reduced by several sizes in any dimension. People should therefore steel themselves against the all-pervading trickery of the International Totalitarian Police State pirates in whose illicit grasp we are. No one should have exploratory operations, or submit to unnecessary surgery, or agree to be irradiated by x- or cobalt rays, or have their teeth out, etc.

Other uses of this heat weapon clearly are: masking, or intensifying the effects of acupuncture; varying the severity of corporal punishment without the person administering it necessarily being aware.

Incendiarism – buildings, ships, planes, space capsules, crops, bush fires, racing drivers. The fire precautions racket is now enormous and premises can be gutted whatever the forced investment in alterations and security. Kohoutek – (who made it?) 'It came from outer space' 'The dinosaurs were wiped out by a meteor'.

Crumbling concrete, stone, rocks, roofs, spires, ancient monuments, coastlines, canal and river banks, Venice, subsidences, avalanches, cracks in rockets, the Russian Concorde that disintegrated, the Welsh tips, pit winding gear that fails, colliery accidents.

Rusting ships, cars, planes, tail units that fall off, metal 'fatigue'.

Fading pictures, flooding Venice, drowning Bangladesh repeatedly, eroding carvings, to make work and get money out of the Public to pay for it.

Inculcating superstition – misleading the Public on the religious plane while making the reality forever unattainable. Lourdes, the Ganges, the faith-healing industry, Christian Science; the real effects wrongly attributed to witchcraft, sorcery, voodoo;

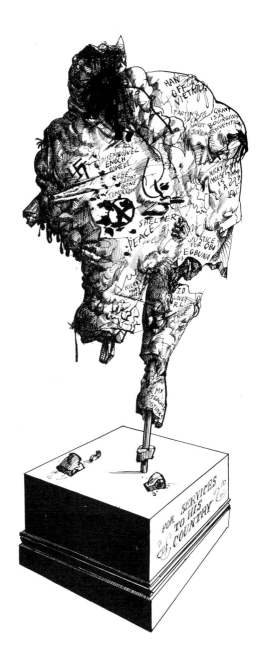

THE PEN IS MIGHTIER THAN THE SICKLE

palmistry and astrology. (Thor is again officially recognised in Iceland with libations of red wine.)

There is nothing wrong with tobacco. Research into filters, carcinogenic effects, and manmade tobacco substitutes, is a gigantic fraud involving the endless mass torture and killing of small animals, and the standing murder of thousands of healthy people. People should be advised that there is NO PRIVACY to be counted on anywhere by day or night thanks to satellites, holographic T/V and infrared, and that this circumstance alone has abolished civilisation. Since we cannot live without privacy, except alone, this must be remedied by concerted public

anger and the Law. It is up to you.

Implants and A.I.D., the need for which is quite artificial, should be avoided like the plague. Individuals are the subject of a world wide game involving miscegenation, and they risk having whatever ingredients of animal, fish, bird, reptile or plant they have personally been given intensified in their offspring.

No one should agree to see a psychiatrist who still retains any freedom of choice. Avoidance is the only certainty of remaining mentally intact, and socially untainted by imputations of one sort or another.

The proper course of action for the Public, if the Government will not, or cannot,

empower the county and metropolitan constabularies to act, is indeed physical – it is military. What, except to defend us, are the Armed Forces of this country for – paid with our money, manned with our men? Nevertheless, faced with a situation that has been contrived to demand the appearance of a new Cromwell, we must not easily be caught in that trap. The Law must at least first be tried. Please contribute realistically towards the spread of this and further information, and a fighting fund for legal expenses.

P.H.D.
14 November 1973

56

57

Heat, by God! The heat. Chunks of it pressing in on every part of your body. Clammy, bored people wandering about the baggage claim. Policewomen with bulging pants stand checking baggage of departing passengers. Everything has a temporary feeling – jerry-built. Frayed at the edges.

Manners change. Some folks take care to be polite but some just couldn't give a damn. We are staying in a reasonably pleasant, hacienda-style motel. The service is curt and to the point. Who's paying the bill? – Straight Arrow – Straight what? – Straight . . . Oh, never mind, if you'd care to call them – That won't be necessary, sir. Do you have a credit card? – No! Blank look. – Well, if you wish to use the bar you'll need this Guest Card. Don't lose it . . . sir!

The bar is dark – the Cuatro Club. Noisy crowd of crazies sitting around a table full of empty Bud beer cans. The room is functional but there it is, life going on. Here – out there – people sit in rooms miles from everyone, living their lives like no one else existed. If one could see all these diverse scenes simultaneously – which is impossible – the world would be positively buzzing with movement.

Dallas is flat and shabby on the outskirts. New buildings have heat-reflecting mirror glass, mainly in gold. The freeways into the city abound with cheap eat-in places which usually stay in business about twelve months, then change hands. Dallas has gone. It disappeared ten years ago, on November 22, 1963.

Now it's a thriving tourist town with a live waxwork museum and the Kennedy Memorial show – nothing else at all except new blocks of high-rise mirror glass and a Hilton on downtown Commerce Street. Our visit happened to coincide with the colourful, jazzy 74th Black Elk Convention held at the Hilton. A lobby full of fat, contented Duke Ellingtons, mamas, comely Stetson-hatted black dollies all plump in the right parts, grandmas, grandpas – wizened, lined little Deep Southern faces straight off the front porches of Alabamie! Big black businessmen showing how they've made it, white style, in their white, diamond-studded fezzes dangling huge gold tassles over their flash off-the-peg gear.

This philanthropic event, run on a non-profit-making basis, was filling up the Dallas Hilton to show off the Elks' achievements and themselves, and to raise money to help more deprived kids (black and white) get an education – and religion. Although

59

the Black Panthers would also like deprived kids to have an education, their philosophies on how to achieve that aim must be sorely different.

The strong, English, middle-class streak in me applauded the almost childlike gaiety, look what we've done, ain't everybody friendly sort of feeling that shone from the gorgeous black faces. I even felt vaguely comfortable and safe among them. Comfortable and safe is their way and that's how they like to make it. And so what, I think their zest outshone the undertones political and social, and that was nice, even though it was a convention – or a show of strength.

Beginning to feel heavy and fat. I now weigh two hundred pounds holding a pizza in each hand.

Walking down Main Street. Lots of weird people – like anywhere, I suppose – we're all weird. It's just that some people have the edge. I can't draw them all so I select. Look for the nice amusing ones. Remember my resolve. Often wish I was a movie camera – catching it all on the spot, and editing later. There's a deep frustration felt when getting something on paper in the middle of a busy street. A longing to record it all but missing about 80 per cent. Like a series of slow burn jokes; before you've got the first one, the next one is on you and so you save up all the laughing for the end. The series of hurried squiggles on the page leaves me hoping that my memory will serve me well later.

Snarling red-eyed dogs began to fight in the centre of the bar room floor as the drug I had taken earlier in the day as a cure for sea-sickness and headache took a hold.

Richard Nixon's brother, I think it was his brother, leaned diagonally against the bar of this quayside waterhole at Newport, Rhode Island, talking to other red-faced yachting men down for the 1970 Americas Cup, and playing no heed whatsoever to the snarling red-eyed dogs I was trying to avoid.

It had been a long strange week afloat in a fifty-foot hired sloop and in the company of my companion, an engaging scourge, Doktor of Gonzo and Sophist in white sneakers called Dr Hunter S. Thompson. A merciless rock group had been hired for the ride (to help us in our work) by *Scanlan's* magazine to get the real story on this famous yacht race and its own kind of redneck enthusiasts. I had always put their red necks down to constant exposure to sea salt but Hunter explained many times that it was more to do with the pressure at the base of the skull. Their brains are lower than most.

Earlier in the week, during a walk along the waterfront, where he had paid particular attention to the positions of the jetties, Dr Thompson had purchased a jack-knife with one of those pig-sticker attachments used by boy scouts the world over for extracting stones from horses' hooves. Dr Thompson had bought one 'just in case'. I didn't bother to ask him why, feeling far too worldly. I had, in fact, been not only a boy scout in my time but a troop leader as well and was therefore perfectly able to assess the possible need for such a piece of equipment. 'Be prepared' is the motto, and the training never leaves you.

Scanlan's magazine, incidentally, for those of you who missed those nine wild months of publishing history when Warren Hinckle III, 61

Newport, Rhode Island – America's Cup 1970 – dress rehearsal for Las Vegas drawings – this assignment was never finished. Hunter Thompson flew back to Aspen to stand for Sheriff – and I went to England full of nightmares...

The rest of the sketchbook was destroyed by salt water + lost. The assignment was never finished

At the Piano

appetites outstripped the financial cornucopia that was there to begin with. After the ninth issue the well dried up and the magazine was no more. We were out on a limb, covering the Americas Cup for the next issue, when that happened. Not the best kind of news to learn over a bad line from New York whilst asking for more funds to dig deeper.

It was *Scanlan's* who found me in Long Island when I had arrived from England one week earlier in April 1970 to seek my particular vein of gold in the land of the screaming lifestyle.

I was about to head for New York anyway to look for work when I got a call from *Scanlan's* art director, J.C. Suares, asking whether I would like to fly to Kentucky and work with an ex-Hell's Angel called Dr Hunter S. Thompson. Undaunted by the credentials and in my innocence, for I am an exceedingly trusting man, I agreed to go, packed my bags and said goodbye to my good friends Dan and Pam Rattiner, proprietors of Dan's Papers in the Hamptons on Long Island, who had so kindly given me a home for the week. I arrived

whose brainchild the magazine was, scorched through three-quarters of a million dollars of borrowed money in a pitiless pursuit of truth – not least the call to impeach Nixon as early as 1970 – was named after a little-known Nottingham pig farmer.

It was a magazine dedicated to maverick journalism and anything that seemed like a good idea at the time. Together with his business partner Sydney Zion, who later gained a reputation as someone who knew a thing or two about psychiatrist Daniel Ellsberg, Warren set about making sure everyone knew everything about anything that moved in America from covert activities in high places to rats in a New York restaurant kitchen.

Needless to say, they achieved their goal and made Nixon's enemy list in record time, but unfortunately Warren's excessive lifestyle and

in New York at the 42nd St offices of *Scanlan's* monthly, conveniently placed above a cosy bar serving Irish Guinness and flanked by dark doorways of the most unsavoury kind.

J.C. Suares greeted me with some caution as I remember, treating me rather like a hired hit man with a certain reputation which had arrived ahead of me.

It was some time later that I learned that I had not been a get-Steadman-at-any-cost kind of choice. Hunter had suggested Pat Oliphant, then of the *Denver Post*, whom he'd got to know locally, when he first thought of the Derby piece.

Oliphant, as it happened, was off to London to attend a cartoonist's convention and had declined the invitation to be Hunter's sidekick.

I have to thank him or hate him for that, though he saved my first trip to America from being a total washout.

I was introduced to the editor, Donald Goddard, a kindly shrewd man and an ex-foreign editor for the *New York Times* who had picked up a book of my collected cartoons in England, *Still Life with Raspberry*, the very week I left for America.

Don explained in a little more detail and with reserved reassurances how interesting this job might prove to be. Being an Englishman himself he set my natural anxiety at ease as could only another Englishman who is far from home but armed with foreknowledge.

On the way to the airport I stopped off at Don's apartment where I met his wife, Natalie, a rep from Revlon, which was fortunate, you see. I had left my inks and colours in the taxi and was therefore, as far as an artist is concerned anyway, naked. Miraculously, Natalie had dozens of samples of Revlon lipstick and make-up preparations which solved the problem in one stroke. They were the ultimate in assimilated flesh colour.

Finding Hunter, or indeed anyone who was not a bona fide registered journalist covering the prestigious Kentucky Derby, was no easy matter. Trying to explain my reasons for being there was even more difficult, especially as I was under the impression that this was a bona fide trip anyway and I was an accredited press man. Why shouldn't I think that? I assumed *Scanlan's* was an established magazine. As it turned out, *Scanlan's* had just about got me the hotel room at an awful jerry-built complex called Browns.

From there on in I was on my own. Innocence and an English way of asking directions, coupled with a look of utter bewilderment, stood me in good stead. I noticed this early on and acquired a knack of looking more bewildered, more innocent and more English if things got hairy, though having said that I have probably blown my cover for any future assignment. Not being able to locate Hunter at the hotel, although he had booked in, I decided to take myself off to the track,

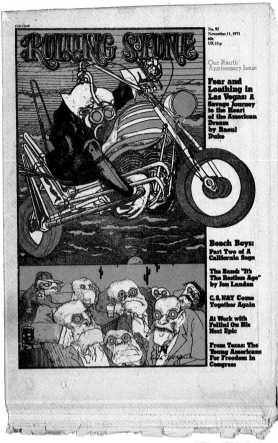

eager to see the colour and excitement I had been led to expect. I carefully selected a sketch book, a couple of handy felt-tip pens and a camera.

I had imagined in my naive way, something like a New Orleans Jazz Carnival or a set from *Carousel*. The first impression gave me a shock. People jockeyed and shoved for positions in an uncertain queue. (Not the most American of institutions. I suspect it probably reminds them of the Depression queues of the 1930s.) I became a piece of flotsam and sensed my foreign politeness cut no ice here.

'I'm looking for the press room,' I said.

'Go buy a ticket,' said the cashier through the ticket office window. 'Dis ain't Ascot, Buddy!'

I paid my way and passed through a green corrugated portal into a tunnel which lead to the centre field where everyone with absolutely no important mission to fulfil sloshed around in a sea of empty beer cans, hot dog stands and obsolete form cards. Some people were camped out with all the mod cons necessary for a comfortable three-day stint. This was carnival centre and not an ounce of influence operated here. These were the Christians waiting to face the lions and the Romans were up there in the surrounding grandstand making bets.

I retreated back the way I'd come, looking around the back of the seat scaffolds until I finally located the stairs leading to the Press Box. With a high charge of English bewilderment I talked myself inside, passed a pleasant lady with a southern drawl and got myself a beer at the bar. From where I stood I could see the course and the finishing posts. Press men were typing away and phoning editors and commentating through mikes to their radio stations. The races were in full swing. I felt heavy with a sense of inadequacy. I couldn't type, I had no one to phone anything to, I knew nothing about racing and I couldn't even locate the man who could probably fill me in and make me feel that I was here for some good reason. It is a feeling I have experienced on many subsequent occasions when I have been shot into the middle of a strange place by some magazine or other which believes that all credentials are bullshit and that the mere mention of their name will send officials into paroxysms of reverence and respect. I suppose it's understandable, as any magazine proprietor worth his salt, with the desperate

AMERICA

Ralph Steadman 79

belief that the whole world is waiting with baited breath for the next issue, must think like that or go under with his circulation figures.

I had been watching someone chalk racing results on a blackboard whilst I finished my beer, and was about to turn and get another when a voice like nothing I had ever heard before cut into my thoughts and sank its teeth into my brain. It was a cross between a slurred karate chop and gritty molasses.

'Er – um, 'scuse me, er – you – er – you wouldn't be from England, would you? Er – an artist – maybe – er – what the – !'

I turned around and two eyes firmly socketed inside a bullet head were staring at the funny beard I was wearing on the end of my chin.

'Er – sorry – I – er – ' the mouth hardly moved, being firmly wedged between two pieces of solid jawbone. 'I – er – thought you might be – er!'

'I *am* from England,' I replied, 'my name's Ralph Steadman – you must be Hunter Thompson.'

'That's right. Where you been? I was beginning to worry. I thought you may've been picked up or something.'

'Picked up?!' I didn't quite understand.

'Yes – er – police here are pretty keen. They tend to take an interest in something different. The beard – er – not many of them around these parts. Er – why don't we grab a beer and maybe talk things over.'

I began to take in this man's appearance and his was a little different too. Certainly not what I was expecting, anyway. No time-worn leather shining with old sump oil. No manic tattoo across a bare upper arm and certainly no hint of menace. No. This man had a pretty impressive head cut from one piece of bone and the top part was

65

The last races were being run and there wasn't much else that could help us around the track so it was decided that we'd return to the hotel, clean up and go into Louisville to eat.

I had so far made no sketches or notes, being far too intimidated to do either, but my head was buzzing with strange impressions.

Hunter had hired a bright red whale of a car and had stowed two buckets of beer on ice behind the front seats. We stopped off at a liquor store and bought more ice and a bottle of Wild Turkey bourbon – a drink I was not yet familiar with. It tasted good and went down even better, though compared to a good malt whisky it's still a rather clumsy way to get drunk.

I was beginning to settle in.

'Maybe we'll just get ourselves organised and we could meet my brother in Louisville – he's expecting us.'

'OK by me,' I said. I was busy watching him drive the car. From the very beginning I could tell he was able to handle a car with considerable skill. He is the sort of driver who can never be a passenger. The left hand holds the wheel, the right hand holds the cigarette holder and a beer can. Between his legs he keeps a tall glass full of ice and whisky. The consumption of each item is carried out in nervous progressions: the cigarette holder with lighted cigarette is placed in the mouth, drawn on and taken out. Then, with the same

covered down to the eyes by a flimsy white tight sun-hat. The top half of his main corp was draped in a hunting jacket of multi-coloured patchwork and the bottom half wore slightly too-small seersucker blue pants. The whole was supported by a pair of huge white plimsolls with fine red trim around the bulkheads. Perfect proportion as a foundation for what looked like a lot to support. Damn near 6 feet 6 inches of solid bone and meat carrying a beaten-up leather bag in one hand and a cigarette in a holder in the other. His eyes gave away nothing of what he thought he was looking at in me. (A matted-haired geek with string warts, but this opinion only became known to me later. Writers have a compulsion to tell all eventually, particularly journalistic ones whose only real reason for being a journalist is to blast out secrets they are entrusted with 'off the record' and surprise the world – or their editors anyway.)

'Maybe we should watch a race or two – get the feel of things. I used to live in Louisville so this is my stomping ground. I could fill you in a bit,' he suggested.

We took seats directly overlooking the race track and I opened my sketch book and relaxed with a beer. Hunter had a note-book and made sporadic notes in red ink.

'Do you bet?' he asked.

'Well, I once put two shillings on Early Mist in the Grand National in England back in 1951 and won at ten to one.'

'Mmm, maybe you should try again. You sound lucky!'

A race was about to begin so we chose a horse just for fun to see how we made out, without spending a cent. The horse won, so we decided to try again for real.

Unfortunately the luck had run out and a modest amount of *Scanlan's* expenses disappeared within the hour.

During that time we had sounded each other out and overcome first impressions. We seemed to be getting along fine. He kept pointing out faces that for him represented the real Kentucky face.

66 'That's what we're here for,' he would say. 'Nail that and you have it.'

hand holding the beer can, he drinks. For a moment the left hand comes off the wheel which is held briefly with the other while the whisky is swigged and put back down. Then the driving hand is returned to the wheel and all this is carried out whilst the car is turning corners or overtaking in the fast lane.

The alternative is for me to hold the wheel whilst he does all these things in quick succession before taking over again. When taking corners the driving hand swivels the wheel in one motion to a magic point on its circumference and the car follows the direction of the front wheels, whatever the speed. It has to. Some divine intervention keeps it on the road. We needed to eat.

I was befuddled by this time and the potent combination of watery beer and whisky was bringing on a severe attack of drawing. This always happens when I start seeing unusual things through a haze of controlled drinking. My body becomes a protective casing and leaves me to observe through two keyholes in the front of my head . . .

'Fuck the story. At this point there *is* no story. I grew up here. I went away and I came back. You appeared on the scene with this stuff like some kind of travelling priest peddling your twisted morality.' It was now one week later.

'I'm just trying to do my job.'

'You miserable . . . That's what Hitler said. Shit.'

Hunter had brought his fist down on the omelette set out for him in the coffee bar where we sat. I feebly wiped at the scrambled substance sticking to my already crumpled sports jacket in an attempt to lessen the shocking effect this would add to the already alarming countenance I had developed in a week.

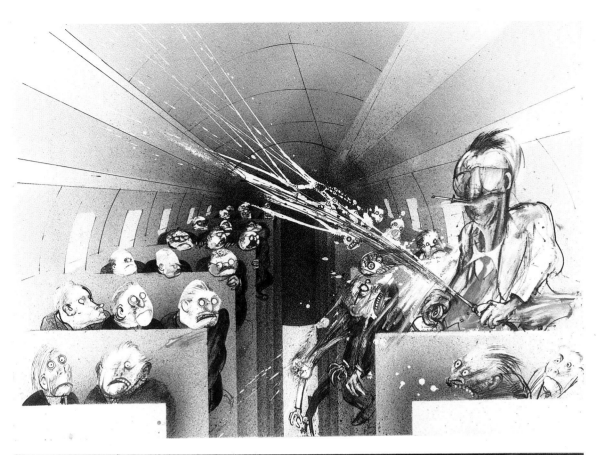

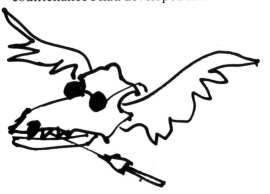

When I think of Hunter Stockton Thompson, I inevitably think of Richard Milhous Nixon.
They are inextricably linked in my brain and perhaps inside my undernourished soul.
They seem to have been at the hub of my reason for such a long time yet Nixon was a part of my life for hardly three years. Perhaps it was Hunter who kept him alive for his own strange reasons though let's not give him too much of the credit for that. Perhaps Nixon himself had his own ideas about staying around. He had, after all, reached that plateau of infamy to which only a handful have ever plummeted throughout history – the rare group of men and women who could look confidently in the shaving mirror each new day and greet themselves with the salutation 'Good morning, Statesman'.
Hunter could never do that – and come to think of it, neither could I.

The few vacant patrons who had ventured into this Second World War concrete bunker-like coffee shop for masochistic reasons known only to themselves were feverishly finishing their respective beverages as they fumbled for ten-dollar bills that would amply cover their tabs without having to wait around to pay at the desk. The scene was getting ugly and ten dollars was, I expect, a cheap price to pay for the preservation of the clothes they were endeavouring to sneak out in and anyway, the cash till and the proprietor himself were covered in the stuff so getting change would have been a messy business.

I eyed the proprietor nervously, expecting him to reach for the phone – Hello, is dat the police? Some maniac has just sprayed my coffee shop with omelette . . . What kind of omelette? Well, there's tomato on da wall mirror and dis is mushroom on da phone here and dis looks like a piece of red pepper on da cash register. It's probably da Spanish omelette, officer – what – yeah – dey're delicious – what time do we – ? Well, we usually stay open till midnight . . .

It was only the excruciating stinging in my eyes that snapped me out of my day-dream. I heard Hunter raving on as I stumbled helplessly about trying to collect up my drawings and baggage.

'I've wanted a worthy cause to try out this chemical billy on all week and now I've found it, you scumsucking geek. That's it. Chew on that for a while.'

I choked and ripped at my shirt in an attempt to stop the fearsome stuff burning my skin. My flailing hands caught something – a beer can – and I tilted the contents over my face and chest to relieve the suffocating pain. I screamed with relief but then the pain returned.

'Arrrrgh. Air, I need air – outside – '

A hand gripped my coat and shoved me forward violently. The clammy heat of the midday sun intensified the burning and the bubbling hot tar

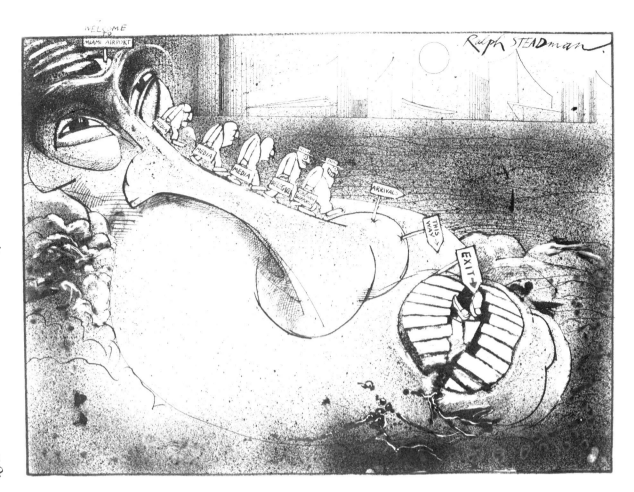

Experts disagree as to whether his complex was the result of an early stage of Parkinson's disease or neuro-syphilis caught during his student days. Neuro-syphilis has hallucinatory effects on the victim, giving him a sense of grandeur, a hatred of humanity, near impotence and, finally, premature senility. At the time Mr Nixon was a student it would have been impossible for him to contract such a disease except perhaps accidentally from a lavatory seat. He died senile at the age of eighty-six in an anti-environment shelter near Camp David, seated before a sun-lamp in a deck-chair wearing only a pair of jackboots.

Isn't that what this country's about? That little Jap?

All the good guys go to law school. Kalmbach. Ehrlichman. Haldeman. Nixon. Segretti. Loyalty is the name of the game.

Ehrlichman – he leaves no more blood on the floor than he has to.

of the car lot outside scalded the palms of my hands.

'My drawings – where are my drawings? I can't see.'

'I've got your drawings, you worthless faggot. Get in the car – you're causing a scene. Do you want to end up in jail?'

There was no sympathy in Hunter's voice now. It was as cold and hard as a municipal sewer pipe. I crawled into the car and grabbed wildly for the ice bucket I knew was behind Hunter's seat, splashing the still cool water over me with a cupped hand.

'Mind the seats, goddamn it. This is a rented car.'

The water momentarily eased the searing sting and I felt the car roar forward as Hunter threw it on to the freeway.

'I'm taking you to the airport, though God knows why I should try and save your wretched little ass. If you weren't a weird stranger around here I'd let them hurl you in jail but I don't need you on my conscience.'

'Thanks,' I said, and put my head inside the bucket which was now on my knee.

'Water doesn't help either,' he said. 'Luckily you only got a mild dose. Apart from losing your eyelashes and three layers of skin you'll be right as rain when you reach New York, though explaining your appearance to airport police might be a little difficult.'

'Oh, don't worry,' I said, 'my skin is allergic to the stifling humidity of tropical swamps like this one anyway. I'm surprised I haven't felt like this sooner.'

I cleaned up in the aircraft toilet during the domestic flight and on arrival in New York made my way straight to *Scanlan's* 42nd St offices to lodge a complaint. The offices were closed and I took a beer in the bar downstairs whilst I wrote a covering note for the drawings to explain the oil stains from the

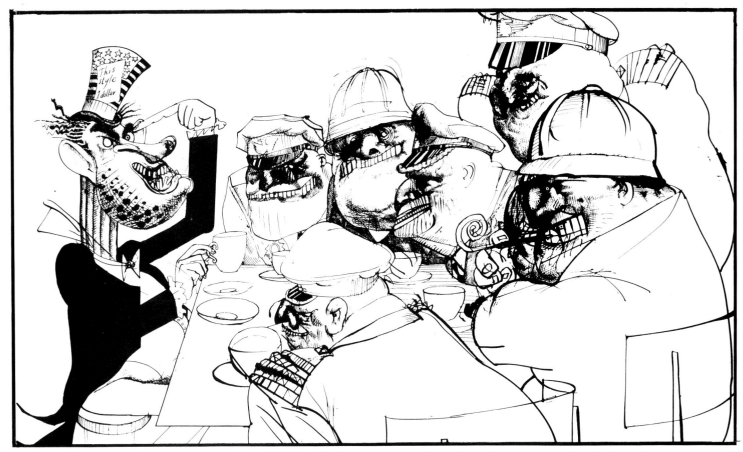

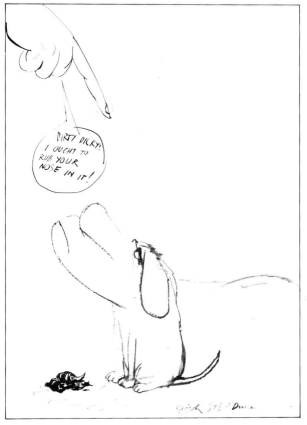

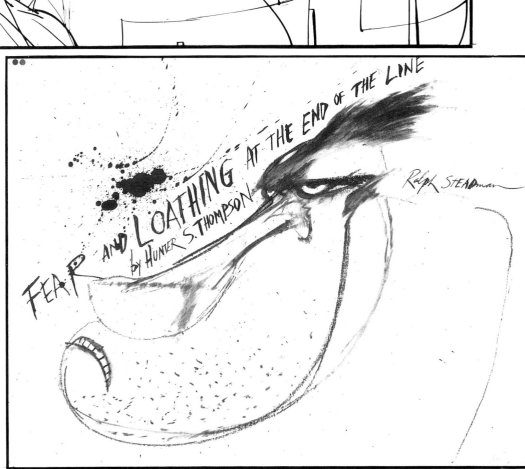

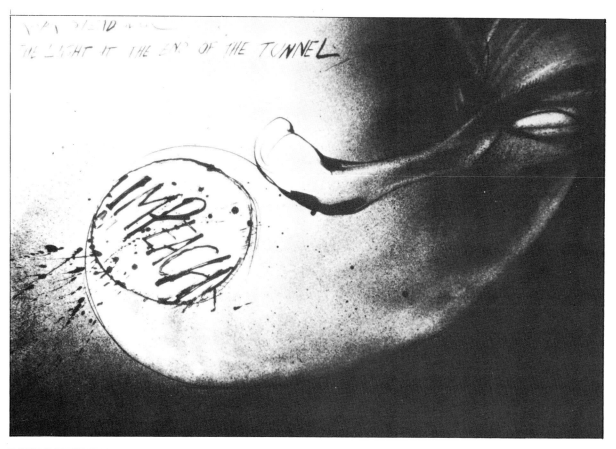

omelette and the reek of the cosmetics I had used to colour them.

I made my way back to the flat I was staying at on West 11th St in Greenwich Village and collapsed on to the bed.

I was awoken from my deep torpor by the phone. It was Warren Hinckle III, *Scanlan's* editor.

'Yeah?'

'Hey, Steadman, is that you?'

'Er – yes – did you get my stuff?'

'You're a messy worker, Steadman – I like it. Lemme ask you – didn't you see any horses?'

'Quite a few.'

'Den why ain't we got any?'

'Ah that, yes, well I'm doing the horse one today.'

'Okay, lemme see it. And whatd'you do to Hunter? He says he can't write and he's blaming you for arresting his creative flow.'

'I'm sorry, he seemed to have personal problems to overcome. Home town, past memories, meeting old friends, that kind of thing. I'm sure he'll produce something soon.'

'Didn't you two hit it off or sumptin'?'

'Like a house on fire,' I said. 'I'll be along to the office just as soon as I finish this horse drawing.'

I rang off and stood silently for a minute or so, staring blankly at the shaking right hand I had raised to wipe the sweat from my brow. It was early May 1970 and the heat was beginning to build up in New York.

On the radio they were playing 'Let it be' and *Scanlan's* magazine was already screaming for the impeachment of Richard Milhous Nixon.

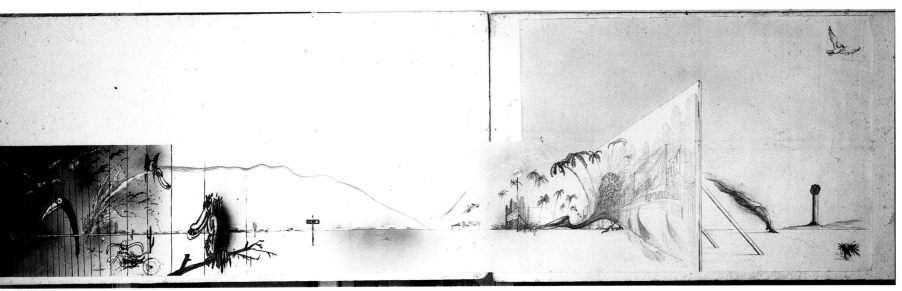

AUSTRIA: I chose AROSA

I look upon skiing as a confirmed teetotaller looks upon a confirmed alcoholic – with shocked fascination. Skiers are drug-addicts whose drug is the white powder they glide over on long flat spoons.

The ski town Arosa itself is pleasant and nestles inside a breathtaking panorama of peaks in the grand Swiss manner. As a friend of mine once said, when confronted for the first time with this endless succession of greater and grander omnipotence – God! I hate Nature.

The town really began to take off when a Doctor Herwig discovered that Arosa had the perfect combination of shelter from wind, invigorating clean air and sunshine. He decided to open a sanatorium for pulmonary diseases and from 1880 to 1900 this became *the* place where the fatally rich preferred to go to be seen dying or dead.

After the Second World War, money poured in as speculators and contractors anticipated a gilt-edged future. They were right – inflation is currently 0.05 per cent per year! Today iridescent furs

protecting well-kept Swiss families glow down the High Street, rubbing shoulders with the *haute couture* of the monied heights in ski boots, gold-plated zips, spikes and sharp edges lancing in all directions. It is wise to walk in the gutter and let them through on their way to the training slopes.

Some of the pupils look no bigger than a full-sized ski boot. They fiddle with their equipment, gaze in every direction but the instructor's and somehow learn to ski, happy in the knowledge that the whole damn family ski, so everything will be all right. Half an hour later you see a one-foot-high figure pitting his newly acquired skills against the odds. One minute the figure stands poised and serene and the next – well, God knows what happens to it. What's one foot in eight thousand seven hundred and four?

I should imagine that to be a Swiss child who does not want to ski must be like belonging to the Masons but not knowing the handshake or being a Yorkshire lad who does not want to go down the mines. Like surfing, skiing is a religion. From grandfather to baby Tobler they tramp up any ski resort high street, ceremoniously dressed in regulation outfits like tailored balloons.

All is vanity, but a ski stretcher

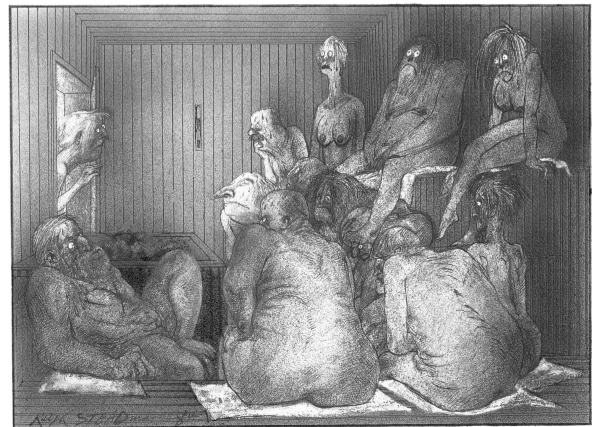

75

Ralph STEADman 74.   *Walking up the High Street to the Hornlii Ski lift.*

propped against a wall inside the ski lift station high up on the Hörnlii peak reminded me that I must curb my Philistine churlishness and appreciate a little of the sport's heroic spirit and the courage of a soul who pits himself against a mountain's treacherous contours. Having done so, I strapped my shame tightly in the stretcher and sent it on its way, then I climbed inside a cable car, its sole occupant, to descend safely and thoughtfully.

Walking Skis.

Ralph Steadman 71   Hörnlii Cable Car.

BERLIN

I clung to the walls as I turned the corners of the burnblack city. The fine misty rain brushed my face like a damp gossamer flannel.

Berlin – damn! And on a wet Wednesday afternoon too – half day closing. I wish I'd never *heard* of the place, or the job for that matter.

I wasn't even sure if de Predis would show up.

For an instant, life's timeless uncertainty was caught in the driving mirror of some passing milk float.

I started.

'Stogdon! Never!! Not here. Could it . . .?' There was only one way to find out . . .

81

HONG KONG

KOWLOON WALLED CITY

Having visited the library in the Hong Kong City Hall to fill my mind with vital information regarding the evil traps in store for the unwary, and full of fear and apprehension, I took the ferry to the mainland and the city of Kowloon. Here vice is so intense that even getting a haircut can be the beginning of a night to remember.

I took the No. 5 bus uptown to the area known mainly for its market place, the screaming of jets bearing down hard on Kaitak Airport four blocks away and the dark and sinister Walled City, headquarters of every fragmented group of the Triads (Chinese Mafia) who run the whole area. The Walled City is the seat of Hong Kong's unofficial government and the home of every vice known to man from buggering twelve-year-old blind girls to mah-jong. I decided to move surreptitiously into the area wearing a blue denim safari jacket and jeans, three Pentax cameras, a Pan Am shoulder bag, two-tone lace-up brogues and a Norwich Union insurance policy. Cleverly anticipating trouble I had left my wallet at the hotel and carried only a modest sum of Hong Kong dollars in the front pocket of my jeans. Somehow I was determined to brazen it out and walk into the area marked with savage red signs saying Crown Property Keep Out.

I stopped at a mangy café next to one of the tunnels which led into the interior, and asked for a beer. The commotion caused by such a request from a westerner resulted in my being asked to join a group of Chinamen for lunch. They sat in the street at a table by their truck. I blanched for a moment at the sight of food on the pavement. Their kindness was touching and I enjoyed a selection of the most extraordinary fish dishes and chop suey. An old man sat squatting

ALLEY WORKSHOPS
Ralph Steadman

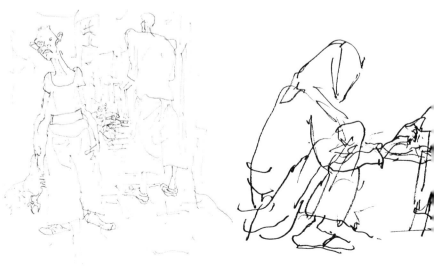

Hong Kong Urban Development

83

CROWN
NO [...]

KOWLOON
WALLED CITY
ENTRANCE

Ralph STEADman

on the café step cleaning fish. The meal was delicious and I stopped eating only when one of my chop sticks fell into a gutter running with water used to clean the fish. My chance to enter the Walled City came when I befriended a tiny kitten tied with white silk to a chair leg under a pile of boxes and mat rushing all somehow connected to a stall selling incense. An entrance lay wide open for my meandering approach so I began to walk in, waiting for someone to challenge me. Nobody did and I continued to walk.

The smell of open drains made my nose twitch. The floor beneath my feet was uneven and dirty. Channels of filthy water gurgled and slurped and ran up, down and around. Dental shops with bright windows full of junk plastic gums and silver braces holding grinning teeth of all sizes glittered in marked contrast to the dark twisted alleyways slinking off in all directions. Huddled next to a dentist one would find a dried fish stand, greasy, dark and smelly with men playing mah-jong and checkers in open doorways. Plumbing and electrical circuits covered the walls amidst endless collages of corrugated iron, old bamboo, string, metal sheet, cement stucco and faded Chinese advertising signs. Glimpses through doorways revealed tiny rooms containing beds cluttered with bric-à-brac and dirty linen. Stopping only rarely and trying to keep some sense of direction from one end of the city to the other, I relaxed a little and found much gentleness in the shadowed faces. The most broken down figures seemed full of worldly wisdom, as though they'd seen it all before – except me, who stood out like a Hilton Hotel. But I didn't appear to represent a threat, nor they to me, and I made a friend fairly quickly – a boy with a pigeon cradled in his arms. He followed me through the lanes like a protector.

I tried to walk like Clint Eastwood, hands and cameras at the ready, working for a fistful of dollars. What I wouldn't give for a bumbling stumble through one of those wretched doorways into God knows what.

All surfaces are at crazy angles. Nothing is straight, nothing save the dental shops looks clean. Grubbiness hangs like a tapestry over everything. And, amongst the squalor, men work. They hammer metal, weld, weave, spin rope, make shoes, clear rubble and start to build. The women wash clothes, dry fish, make egg noodles, cook young dogs and eat fresh lice. Washing hangs down from every horizontal spike or ledge. Walls are only made solid by covering every crevice, crack and hole with a piece of cardboard, tin, wood, sacking or fuse box. Squatting figures, together with hens, cats, dogs and rubbish, litter any surface flat enough to support them. And the drains continue to flow; concrete is smeared rather than laid around corners, guiding the water around twisting canals, under rough duck boards and down black holes taking with it vegetable pickings, fish heads, soapy substances and unidentified objects best left to disappear. The sun filters through into grotto-like junctions in the pathways and lights up more crouching figures darkly preoccupied with secretive twitching pursuits.

Many turnings end in awesome cul-de-sacs which lead into a world littered with objects and wizened faces peeping over rough counters in the dark. I look for light. Ways out are suggested by an upward turn in a tunnel but I chance my arm by turning back in again, shuddering with fascination as one does looking into a tin of maggots.

I leave without warning. I breathe a little sigh and look for somewhere to buy a beer. Finding a bar is impossible. I manage to buy a large bottle taken from a non-working fridge filled with water to keep the contents cool. Before I drink I wipe the mouth of the bottle with the inside of my coat. I stand on the pavement trying to look nonchalant and put the bottle to my lips slowly and deliberately and wonder if I will ever have the guts to go back after midnight. But that's another story . . .

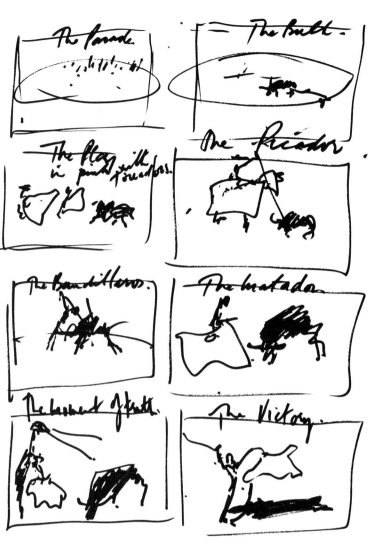

The Little Tin Bullring

Crowds build up around the local tin bullring in Puerto Real, a small town just outside Cadiz. 6.30 pm., June 8, 1983.

Tiny ring/side of railway track/colour of ring traditional. Brownish red/reddish brown?

Horse for the picador/kitted out in armour covering to protect – mainly against bull's horns. Cheap sweets and savoury knick-knacks. Children in Sunday best. Box-offices/holes in perimeter of the bullring cut straight out of the tin. Above some 'sol', others 'sombra'/'sol y sombra' above the rest.

Tickets range from 200 to 3,000 pesetas. The nearer you are to El Presidente the more expensive and the more in shade.

Horses are anchored to the side of the ring. Two more Arab horses/tethered to metal pylon carrying power lines/bull wagon parked hard against guillotine gate set in tin perimeter/clumping of hooves inside. Buy a medium-price ticket costing 700 pesetas – 'sol'. It's half an hour before fight/seats still empty. Seat high up/close to section barrier.

Vendors with usherette trays/scrambling/selling crisps, popcorn and chewing gum. No beer. Sunday evening.

Sun is not strong. Nobody wearing a hat. The place is beginning to fill up/excited children/ killing ritual/extension of Sunday school.

Forgotten what to expect/1959 when I last saw bullfight. Ring smaller than expected, even for local one. Big rings Seville, Malaga, Estepona.

Popcorn sellers clambering over legs/hunched shoulders/ sales

pitch hots up. Chewing gum to keep my mouth fresh/get some queer looks as I mumble into small tape recorder. Sunday evening out/strangers are noticed.

Sol side of ring nearly full. More in *sol* section than *sombra*. Not that *sombra* side protects you from much. Ring very shallow/band tuning up/officials wandering, looking lost, trying to be important. People clap/tension mounts. Fifteen minutes to go/ sun behind cloud but still hot on the head. Long for hat. Banderillero spears, pretty pink, acid green and yellow. Spanish ladies dressed in flamenco dresses seated directly above the tunnels where bulls will exit – dead. Getting closed in here. Boy on bench above shading me from worst of sun/my balding scalp stinging.

Five minutes to go. Impressive hats in tunnel – one or two police, couple of military ones, no toreadors or matadors yet. People clapping and shouting across the ring/can't possibly hear, let alone see. Check. Sketch book, tape recorder and three cameras. Ready.

Right on time/band strikes up. Gates open beneath El Presidente. A strut of six matadors/sleek black costumes/coats cut short to waist/emerges from tunnel/followed by man on horseback/wearing grey Spanish hat, blue-grey coat, protective leather leggings. Tour of the ring, waving, clapping and cheering/then back inside tunnel.

Immediately bull rushes out of another tunnel just below me to my right/looks for business. A torment of toreadors appears from behind barriers carrying pink and yellow cloaks/tempts bull from all sides/tires bull/provides practice for young matador. Preparatory stage/bewildered bull. Not surprising. Prodded and shoved from inside a dark container, along narrow tunnel/out into bright, sandy ring encircled by bobbing heads, cheering and bad music for no apparent reason.

Picador emerges, riding a horse and carrying a lance. On this occasion his costume is fairly rudimentary. Button waistcoat, short jacket and metal leg-protectors. The horse has its armoured skirt – metal sown into quilted eiderdown. The picador wears 'gorblimey' flat peaked cap.

Towers above the bull, jockeying for position where he can best strike the animal in the back of the neck with a lance. Toreadors divert the bull's attention/reduce the danger of full frontal attack. Note: the horse is blindfolded. Picador wounds muscles along the top of the shoulders/forces the animal to drop the weight of its head for the matador to begin ritual of humiliation. Toreador on a horse is traditionally unpopular/heavy mocking from the crowd.

After picador the banderilleros/possess enormous courage. They must jab two gaily-coloured sticks into either side of the first wound.

Banderillero moves deftly – leaps aside like lightning after his strike. Risks a mainline thrust from a bull's horn and a lifetime of ruin. That's why many Spaniards have such a funny walk.

Bull now bleeds profusely from the top of its neck.

Prancing toreadors try the bull's patience persistently. Matador stands behind protective fence on ring's perimeter. Watches bull's characteristics noting strange quirks or movements.

The bull is nearly ready now/real mad/prime energy blunted by wounds/rushing around the ring. Toreadors continue to play him and await the matador. Arrival heralded by the band. They have

attempted thus far to keep up with the action/like old-time cinema pianist trying to follow a silent movie.

Enter the matador. At all times he adopts arrogant posture whether he feels the weight of the bull on his backside or avoids it. Depending on experience and natural aptitude these postures can be extremely elegant. In some cases beautiful.

The *muleta* red cloak is wheeled about in figures of eight or straight sweeps. The performance can be as long or as short as the bullfighter decides. He must dominate the beast, tire it by its own charges until the bull is so mesmerised it stands for long moments in stupor. Matador struts, shouting and taunting. The bull charges again and again. The matador touches its horns. Arranges the bull's head mockingly, then turns. Walks away/back to the creature/displays his lack of fear/control of the confrontation.

He prepares the bull for the moment of truth which can be the quickest or the messiest moment in the contest. Bull breathes convulsively. The matador entices one or two more charges, depending on crowd reactions and the position of sun in relation to the matador and bull, which should look into the sun. Goes down on one knee/bows reverently to the bull as a mark of respect – or is it mockery? Ego of the matador now enjoys full flight. Tip of his sword

89

Peter O'Sullivan Talks **TURF**

is held horizontally in front of him, level with the eye. He looks along the blade and takes aim.

The most dangerous moment. The bull knows by now that this man is up to no good. It also senses its imminent death. The matador remains still. The bull seems compelled to do likewise. The slightest accidental twitch will cause the bull to charge with every last nerve, operating on pure survival instinct. The lunge must be quick and should, if accurate, sink up to the hilt into the bull to reach the heart. The matador must be ready to side-step its final violent spasm.

The ineptitude of the matadors I watch is evident. One man makes six attempts before he finally drops the poor wretch with the jab of a hilted tip to the brain. He gets only one ear. Another bull thunders out. It will be dead in twenty minutes. Pounding powerful solid muscle. When the bull is fresh it's a bloody nightmare. Toreadors tantalise it/a 'lighthearted game'.

This one bewilders easily. Banderilleros miss first time. Second one gets him in the side of the neck. Enter the matador with red *muleta*. He shouts and taunts the bull. The band strikes at each new development. His hat blows off. Second bull dies quickly/one shot, straight through to the heart. Matador gets two ears. The third matador made three lunges. It varies. No, four goes! He hasn't

Red RUM

Lester Piggott

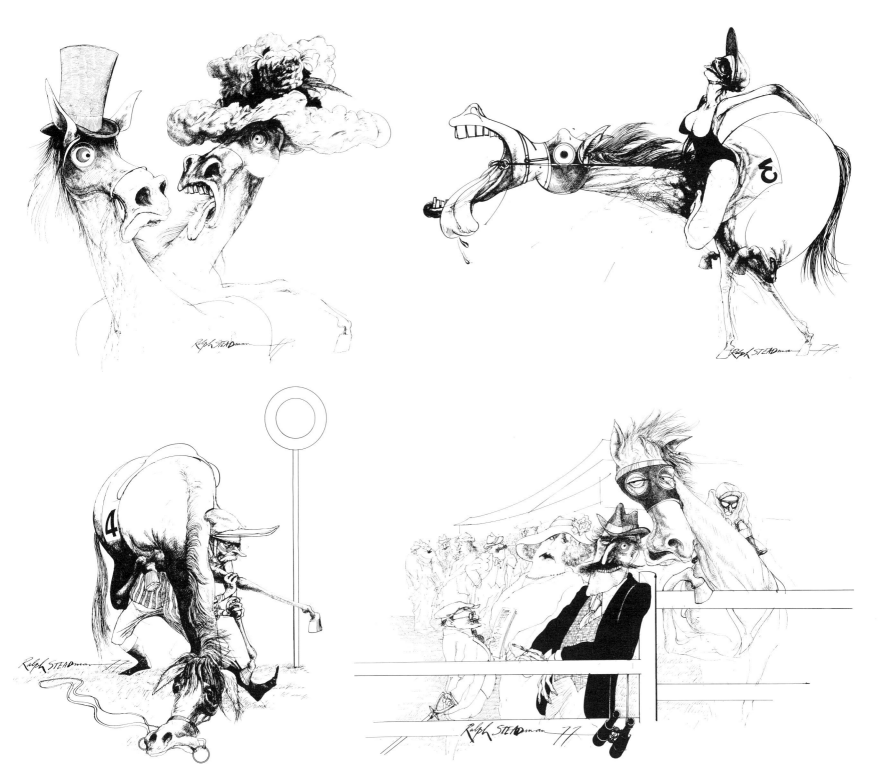

finished yet! Five goes! He's trying for a sixth! Six plunges but the bull stands. Blood spread like plastic sheet on back. The matador calls for another sword. Kills bull in the brain with the hilted tip. Seen enough. 8.10 p.m. – one hour and ten minutes to kill three bulls. Is that good or bad?

Bear in mind this is not a first division show but is small town Sunday afternoon amateur time. Unfortunately they are not playing. Whether they are good at it, or hideously bad, the bull dies. If he *has* to die, better he goes with dignity. The truly awful aspect of the sport is that it can be played by mere beginners who have no other way of learning than simply to get in there and do it. Kill a bull, anyhow. But kill it.

MIDDLE AMERICA

It is several years ago now that I first heard about plans to put Dr Hunter S. Thompson on the big screen. Naturally I was appalled. King Kong, yes. Godzilla, well OK. A re-make of *The Thing* or even *It Came From a Sewer on the Dark Side of the Moon* has possibilities, but *Dr Gonzo* was really scraping the bottom. But don't listen to me. I believe that nothing good was ever made after *Intolerance*.

The part of an artist had been written into the script: a man who briefly appears here and there throughout the plot, draws something and goes away. I was now interested.

'Is that me?' I enquired anxiously, hoping I was at last about to taste the juices of international stardom.

'Well, not exactly,' replied Art Linson, the director. 'It's sort of something my scriptwriter, John Kaye, dreamed up, but we may cut it out.'

'Cut it out?' I choked on the words. 'But this is the story of Hunter's life, isn't it?'

'Sure. But it's not merely a documentary,' said Art, 'it's, well – look Ralph, you arrived on the scene in a way that's difficult to fit in. The film really hinges on a relationship. It's a more integral part of what's been happening in America up to Watergate. Stuff like that.'

'Well, I'm in there somewhere. If the third person

is an artist who draws, either it's me or it isn't an artist at all and it's somebody else. It's a perfect cameo part for Robert Redford if it *is* me though. Or I could play myself. Make it cheaper.'

'We'll see,' was Art's hollow reply and my hopes of reaching the big screen were finally dashed when he didn't even pay my taxi fare of twenty-four dollars back to my hotel.

The only other event which has any bearing on my involvement in the film was the creating, writing and performing of a song. Occasionally I pick up a guitar and attempt to play it, why not? It's a very sociable activity. *Rolling Stone* would not exist without it, even if there had been two Richard Nixons, four Spiro Agnews or even four Jann Wenners. Sometimes Hunter gets to know people who have good places to while away an hour or two. (Apart from firing Magnum 44s into mountain sides, he's engaging company.) In one such place there was a guitar and I invited Mo Dean up to meet Hunter. I met Mo after covering the Republican convention in Kansas City in 1976 with John Dean for *Rolling Stone*. Perhaps because Hunter, Mo and I were a strange mix of very different spirits, it was an extremely creative atmosphere for writing a song. I can usually put to music any incoherent set of words strung together. Six hours after we began, we had a song, or the bare words, anyway, and all it needed was a few more stanzas which I wrote later. I knew we had a hit on our hands. That it is not a hit yet is probably my fault.

However, Hollywood twelve

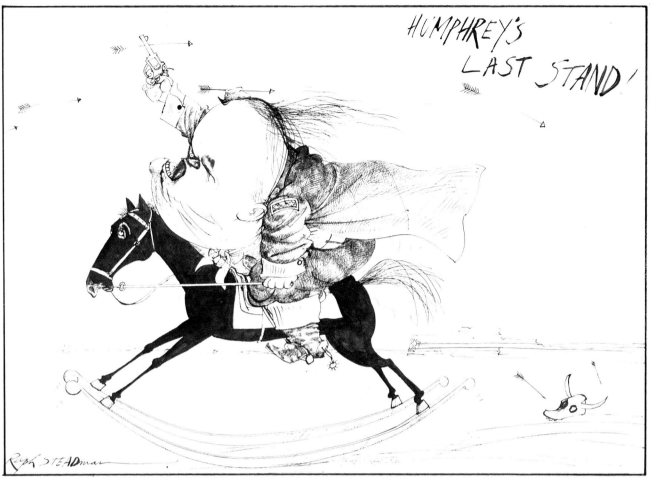

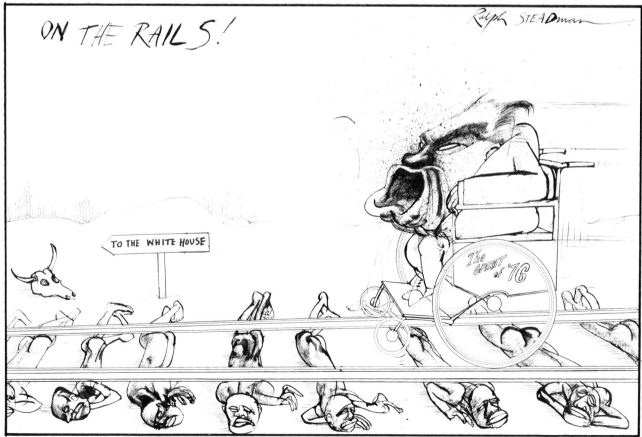

93

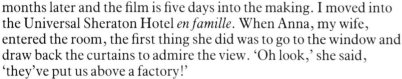

months later and the film is five days into the making. I moved into the Universal Sheraton Hotel *en famille*. When Anna, my wife, entered the room, the first thing she did was to go to the window and draw back the curtains to admire the view. 'Oh look,' she said, 'they've put us above a factory!'

She was referring to the Universal City film lot – a complex of aircraft hangars, sheds and industrial air-conditioning plants overseen by one big black glass tower – the cold heart of the vast Universal Picture Industry.

As Hunter pointed out, on his first day on location in the Piru desert region forty miles out of LA, watching the filming of chickens, they should rename this film *The Death of Fun*.

Watching Art Linson work on the medical scene in a disused Catholic Hospital on the day after I arrived, it was pretty obvious that he was in no relaxed frame of mind to catch the abandoned pure essence of Gonzotic madness which can only happen in uncontrolled conditions. But, with all those Universal millions plus some of his own, no doubt, lying heavy on his shoulders, and enough film to stretch from coast to coast it must be difficult to relax. Better to have exactly one hour and forty minutes of film, a hand-held video recording camera and three dollars in your pocket with a brief that you will be dropped in the middle of Death Valley without anti-snakebite cream, scorpion gun, sun-hat or shades and you must get back to LA in three weeks with the whole lot in the can and ready for a world première first night showing before an awe-struck audience and still have a dollar twenty left. Then and only then do you get your Gonzo initiative and self-reliance badge. Art's sincerity and his fanaticism for the subject he was trying to portray were

95

undoubtedly strong, but blinkered by the idea that the film was a foregone runaway hit.

My opinion was reinforced around the time Hunter decided to take an exploratory walk around the location to relieve the boredom of being an idle spectator. He had absentmindedly walked across a dirty shack window which was part of the scene from inside and which was on camera at the time. Art's voice amplified by bull horn thundered out across the valley: 'Cut! – Get Hunter out of the movie!' If there was ever a perfect Hitchcock cameo, that was it. I don't think it even made the cutting room floor. As far as I know they didn't even print it.

Choosing extras for a film is a heart-rending process. Lined up on the Universal studio campus was the strangest bunch of star-struck hopefuls it has ever been my privilege to gaze upon. A dozen or so were chosen and the rest began to shuffle and look away nervously to hide their disappointment. It was rather touching.

My eyes were still stuck on them. It had to be a drawing at some stage – and did eventually become one. Quite suddenly, my gaze settled on a figure with a Californian walrus moustache who was dressed in a cowboy hat and a patched, rather limp, green two-piece that looked more like snazzy pyjamas.

I pointed him out to Art who was about to move away.

'I think I've found your hitch-hiker,' I said, and pointed discreetly towards the green man. 'That's him.'

'OK,' said Art. 'I'll back your judgment.'

'You bet,' I replied. 'He's got a wooden hand!'

If he ever becomes a star I was the one who snatched him from oblivion, so he can expect a begging letter from me.

With Hunter around, the actor playing him – Bill Murray – began to study him closely. Bill became quiet and introspective. As he once said to me, on the way up to the place Universal had rented for him during the filming, 'I guessed when you hit town, Hunter wouldn't be far behind. Now I'll play Mr Mellow.'

I talked to him about my impressions and observations of Hunter. Especially his mannerisms which are a combination of a swaying forward lurch, nervous rearing twitch and a grimacing clumsiness. A dignified monotone voice lends the whole a certain nobility. Maybe that's a bit kind, but you know what I mean.

If I had to recall one scene which captured the very taste of Hunter's personality it would be the toilet scene in which Bill/Hunter, dressed as Harris from the *Washington Post* in a suit four sizes too small for him, is washing the sweat out of his white tennis shoes when Nixon comes in for a pee. Beating the tennis shoes down on the wash-basin to shake out the excess water Bill/Hunter turns as he realises who has just walked in. He continues to beat his tennis shoes out on the basin, then the wall and finally right on the buttons of two adjacent wall hand-dryers.

Nixon, who appears to be suffering from cystitis, asks how Harris's family is. I saw the rushes and quote from memory.

'The screw heads have got my daughter, sir,' replies Bill/Hunter, beating as he says it, 'and they'll get yours too, sir.' Wap! – 'Well, maybe not Tricia,' Wap! 'but Julie.' Wap! 'They hate Julie, sir' Wap! 'and you, sir,' Wap! – the wet tennis shoes hit the tiled lavatory wall with unforgettable dramatic effect – 'they *really* hate you, sir.' Wap!

Nixon winces at every Wap! and leans his forehead on the urinal mirror.

'And, sir,' continues Bill/Hunter – Wap! – hitting the two buttons of the hand-dryer simultaneously, then hanging the shoes on them to dry off –

'Sir –'

'Yes, Harris?'

'What about the weak, sir, the silly, the dispossessed – the Italians – and, sir –' Bill/Hunter's voice has reached its most poignant, pleading tone.

'Yes, Harris?'

'What about the doomed, sir?'

The index finger of Nixon's right hand beckons Bill/Hunter towards him. He moves forward, his face a portrait of comic sadness.

'Harris – '

'Yes, sir?'

'Fuck the doomed.'

The Vietnam war pinpointed the futility and tragic waste of life that occurs when a major power interferes and becomes embroiled in local ideological struggles for its own pathological reasons, to stem an alien influence. Even more tragically, it has had no effect on the foreign policies of any major power in the East or the West since then because those engaged in their administration can no longer function as rational human beings.

The one positive result, however, has been to distinguish between those who care more for human life than ideologies and those who prefer to pay lip service to a system simply because they are within it, without any regard for whether it upholds a just sense of values based on equal rights for all.

It is for this reason that I find it difficult to support a national cause. My sympathies go naturally toward those who would question motives behind every major political move. Otherwise we have learned nothing.

Gardening Hint No. 49

'Anything to declare?' It was a voice laden with the thick nasal authority of one who knows he has his teeth on the jugular.

'N-nothing!' I replied.

The weight of my spoils was stretching and tearing every joint in my body. I spun around. My bags flew from me in every direction.

'You are aware of your

allowances, of course, sir?' the voice added with mocking respect.

'Er – yes, of course!' I stammered. Damn my greed! I'm always doing it. Six bottles of Jack Daniel's, 2,000 cigarettes, six mahogany boxes of Havanas, French perfume by the pint, an armful of watches, a 12-crate of Chateau Briand '69, four bottles of port and enough Sony transistors to make it worth my while up the North End Road.

I gingerly placed my well-constructed plant-carrying box on the knee-level inspection counter and caressed the petal of a peeping Texas Sage.

'What the blazes is this?' screamed Official Number 2760 C and E. 'Haven't you read the rules?'

'Rules? Oh yes, naturally. Six bottles of spirits, only one crate of wine, only one armful of watches, etc., sure. That's my everything on your floor.'

I'll brazen it out, I thought.

'I'm referring to this,' he said, stabbing a finger into the trembling greenery of my nurtured treasures, which backed off noticeably. 'This is illegal. No flowers or living organism of any kind; no greenery or growing thing, including seeds, corms, bulbs or nurserymen's sundries. Section 402, Subsection 3a, Customs and Excise Regulations 1971, i.e., prevention of disease and virus importation –'

'Disease?! Virus?!' The swine had hit a nerve! 'Have you lost your reason? These plants have no disease. These are the lifelong result of three weeks' intensive tending by sensitive fingers and thoughtful presence. Hark! I could have sworn I just heard the first cuckoo!' I said, wildly trying to change the subject.

'That's the attention bleep for

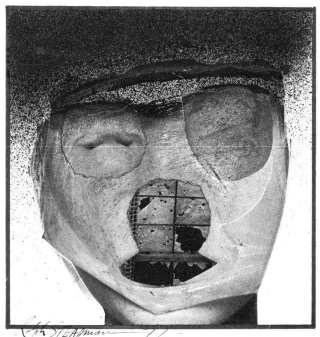

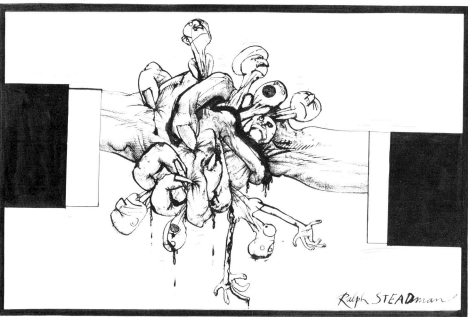

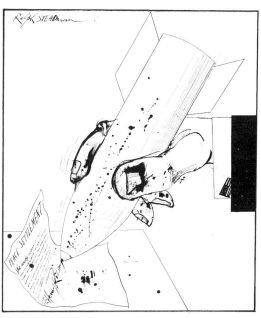

STOP
1984
IN
1976

Demonstration outside
KEMPERARENA K.C. 7 Aug 76
Ralph STEADman

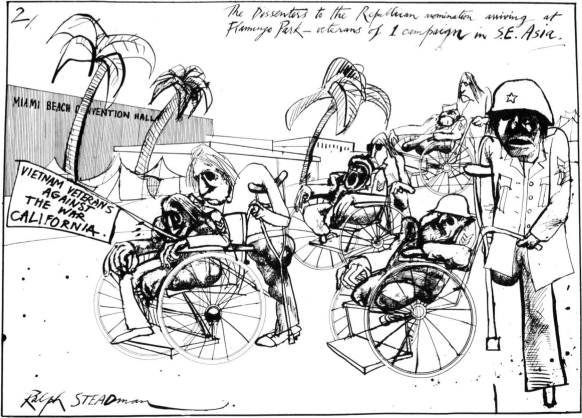

2.

The Dissenters to the Republican nomination arriving at Flamingo Park — veterans of 1 campaign in S.E. Asia.

MIAMI BEACH CONVENTION HALL

VIETNAM VETERANS AGAINST THE WAR CALIFORNIA.

Ralph STEADman

flight information, sir, so if you would step this way I'd like to discuss your position.'

My position was clear and my fingers were already curling around my nicotine azobenzene pocket spray, a sure-fire remedy against the deadly red spider mite, the pest of many plants grown under glass, including melons, grapes, orchids and carnations. In fact, a nicotine spray is an efficient first-aid spray against leaf miners, cuckoo spit insects (wash the spit away before application), gladiolus thrip, aphids, gooseberry mite, mealy aphids, sawfly and ruthless customs officials.

He reeled back, clutching at his eyeballs, giving me enough time to gather up my plants, two bottles of Jack Daniel's, a box of cigars, a bottle of port and a transistor and make an Olympic leap over the barrier into the public zone, losing myself amid a shiny-topped Pentax-swinging Japanese delegation arriving in London for the International Angle-Iron Exhibition at Olympia. Walking on my knees, I was invisible to the outside world. Their charter coach was already ticking over outside Terminal One and I clambered aboard, narrowing my eyes Orientally and settling quickly into the nearest empty seat. My neighbour eyed me through slits.

'Olympia?' I said.

'Ah, so, Olympia,' he replied.

Closing my eyes completely now, I conjured up the sight of two lonely pieces of unclaimed baggage filled as tight as a drum with 57 varieties of sample soil, going around-and-around-and-around-and-around on the baggage claim conveyor of Flight TW 651. Aw hell, I'll claim it on expenses.

A Courtroom portfolio of the Patty Hearst trial. With dialogue by Lewis Carroll.

Alice had never been in a court of justice before, but she had read about them in books . . .

Before she had drunk half the bottle, she found her head pressing against the ceiling, and had to stoop to save her neck from being broken. She hastily put down the bottle saying to herself, 'That's quite enough – I hope I shan't grow any more – As it is, I can't get out at the door – I do wish I hadn't drunk quite so much!'

Alas! It was too late to wish that! She went on growing, and growing, and very soon had to kneel down on the floor; in another minute there was not even room for this. . . Still she went on growing . . .

'It was much pleasanter at home,' thought poor Alice, 'when one wasn't always growing larger and smaller, and being ordered about by mice and rabbits.'

'Consider your verdict,' the King said to the jury. 'Not yet, not yet!' the Rabbit hastily interrupted. 'There's a great deal to come before that!'

'Consider your verdict,' he said to the jury, in a low trembling voice.

'There's more evidence to come yet, please your Majesty,' said the White Rabbit, jumping up in a great hurry. 'This paper has just been picked up.'

'-What's in it?' said the Queen

'-I haven't opened it yet,' said the White Rabbit, 'but it seems to be a letter, written by the prisoner to — to somebody.'

'It must have been that,' said the King, 'unless it was written to nobody, which isn't usual, you know.'

'Who is it directed to?' said one of the jurymen.

'It isn't directed at all,' said the White Rabbit. 'In fact, there's nothing written on the outside.' He unfolded the paper as he spoke, and added, 'It isn't a letter, after all: it's a set of verses.'

'Are they in the prisoner's handwriting?' asked another of the jurymen.

'No, they're not,' said the White Rabbit, 'and that's the queerest thing about it.' (The jury all looked puzzled.)

'He must have imitated somebody else's hand,' said the King.

'Let the jury consider their verdict,' the King said, for about the twentieth time that day.

'No, no!' said the Queen. 'Sentence first – verdict afterwards.'

'Stuff and nonsense!' said Alice loudly. 'The idea of having the sentence first!'

'Hold your tongue!' said the Queen, turning purple.

'I won't!' said Alice.

'Off with her head!' the Queen shouted at the top of her voice. Nobody moved.

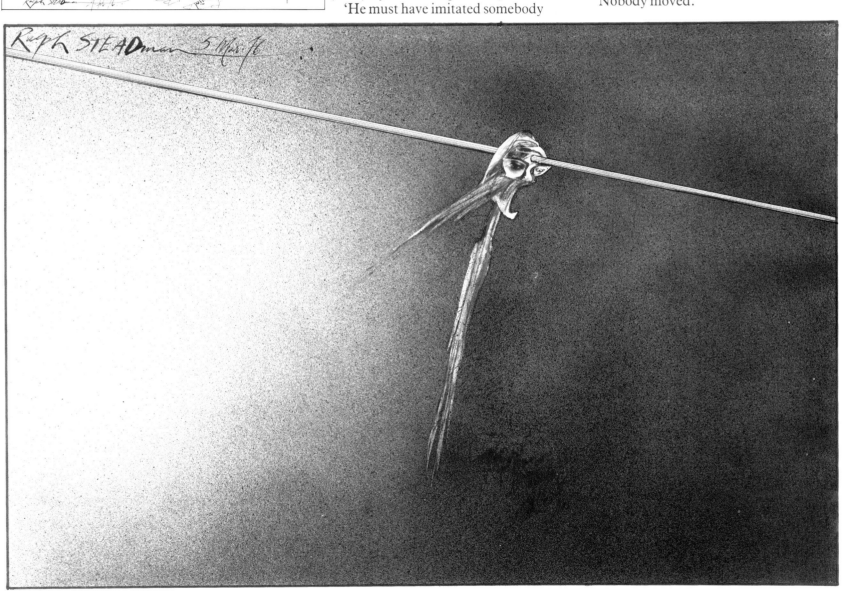

WALLACE'S BIRD OF PARADISE.

Ralph STEADman

VULTURES

Parched with the thirst for something he has no real use for, man staggers on in the desert of his own mess. Vultures are blessed with digestive juices strong enough to break down bones, nylon hooks, shirt buttons and silicon chips but even *they* would not go near the toxic wastes that we spew out across the planet daily. There isn't a vulture low enough to gobble down the graveolent muck that we create – either faecal, chemical or nuclear.

A vulture is an elegant maggot, flying gracefully with a smooth aerodynamic body perfectly suited to gliding at great speed against any wind velocity.

Man is uneasy when a vulture appears on the skyline only because that appearance is usually a manifestation of decay and the farmer who has vultures around the farm will try to destroy them, not because he fears for the safety of his live animals, but because he fears the bad omen that a vulture brings. A vulture will appear before an animal is dead for it instinctively knows when death is imminent. If a farmer can kill vultures, this becomes tantamount to denying the truth, but that can be the only reason for slaughtering the birds because they are not a menace otherwise. If anything they are a blessing in disguise: natural vacuum cleaners who will eat anything and everything, good or bad.

In hot weather, and I mean extreme – 110 degrees in the shade and over – a vulture has been known to shit furiously down its own legs, then take off at great speed. The purpose is obvious. It is an instinctive attempt to cool itself down by the process of rapid evaporation.

As a 25-year member of the Human Observer League I look to the vulture for the new word. A revolutionary vulture culture. How they live may tell us where we are going wrong. If we must pick on the bones of each other then at least let us learn how to do it properly.

1984 – the year of the vulture.

105

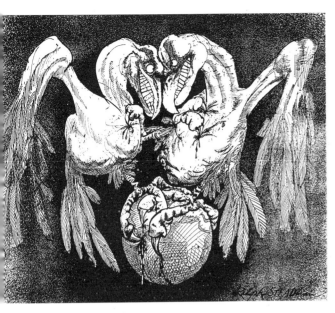

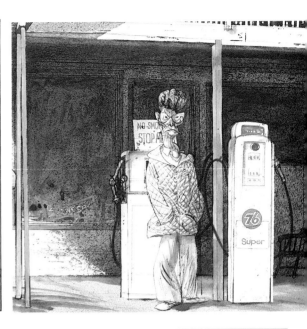

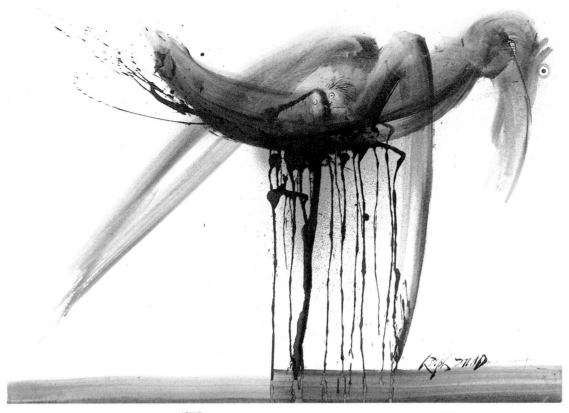

Frazier Park Office, Interstate 5, Freeway to Bakersfield and Sacramento.

7 am. The morning was an absolute delight to wake up to – bright and clear as a crystal vase. There was a pleasant toytown atmosphere about the small town of Frazier Park – a settlement toytown with quaint home-made wooden constructions. Clean atmosphere as we walked to the local rough and ready coffee shop to have breakfast at the counter, shoulder to shoulder with burly, bluff backwoodsmen eating honey-coated pancakes, hash browns with bacon and two eggs over, swilling coffee and telling crude stories of life in the old country.

We got away around 10 am and pointed the car up. We had heard that somewhere along this route into the mountains, or maybe at the top of a mountain, was a condor observation post. The road leading past the Lake of the Woods wound up into the vast mountainous region known as Los Padres National Forest.

There was no clear route to the observation post given on the map and various enquiries produced responses of 'Aw heck, yeah, three guys with glasses always lookin' for condors – ways up there, ya see 'em,' but no precise directions, so we drove on up through pine forests along a meandering road which occasionally forked. We always took the right fork as it seemed to lead upwards. Apart from some rather exclusive looking lodge clubs and compounds with notices stating things such as 'tennis shoes only' or 'members only', or 'private land, no hunting or fishing', most of the land was wild and unspoilt.

Eventually we caught glimpses between the ranges of a promised land stretching out. Stranger still, this appeared to be white with blue mountains on the far horizon. It looked like a white lake.

The petrol gauge was below half full and I was a little anxious at this point that we were getting into pretty desolate terrain. Unless there was one of those lonely gas stations standing isolated like something out of an Edward Hopper painting, we could be in trouble.

A lonely life and one to suit only a very particular temperament. The kind of temperament that would probably survive a nuclear attack.

107

and then turn back and coast down the mountain to conserve petrol. We were convinced at this point that (a) we had passed the condor observation post and (b) we weren't going to see a condor or even a turkey buzzard today. So we stooged for two miles until we came upon a junction. One direction pointed to Santa Barbara on Route 33, and the other to Sacramento on 166. Yet both roads seemed to be part of the same Route. We stopped and considered the situation.

Anna noticed the tip of a gas station sign 77 just over the brow of a rise on Route 166 and we turned right towards it. It looked like something right out of an Andrew Wyeth painting: a white painted weatherboard hut with a front window full of old signs, including one lit Budweiser advertisement, some old tyres and a barking dog.

There was a 'switch off engine, no smoking' sign on one of the pumps and darkness within the windows. Suddenly the door opened and a Wyeth woman proper came out. She was dressed in flared slacks, slippers, a blue quilted plastic jacket and a frilly necked blouse with a cameo brooch over the top button. Her face was as craggy as a reptile's. She wore thin-frame large spectacles and her hair was bunched up into plaits over her forehead like a charlady's headscarf. She was smoking a cigarette which hung from the corner of her mouth and she looked as tough as good leather.

'Yeah?' she enquired.

'Oh – er – unleaded gas please, better fill her up. Will it reach?'

'Sure.' She had already grabbed the petrol hose and was coming around the back of the car as though she had a weapon in her hand.

'Do you know of a condor observation post around here?'

'You mean that place manned twenty-four hours a day watching them damned condors? Sure do. It's ways back there. Where ya from?'

'England.'

'That doesn't help me! Where d'ya come from now?'

One sight I was not ready for was the back view of a carrion crow taking off from a piece of fencing post clutching a rather threadbare small dead bird. I hadn't got a camera ready and the carrion crow had gone before I could even reach for one.

The herds of cattle – mainly brown and black stock – grew more frequent and every building we saw gave us fresh hope that we had found the observation post. Each time the building turned out to be a rancher's lonely home. This is the toughest kind of solitude I can imagine, bar living in a lighthouse.

We were getting more anxious by the minute since we seemed to be passing the point of no return as far as petrol was concerned and Sadie, my nine year old, was getting less inclined to stretch her legs when we stopped to survey the land. We decided to go on for another mile or two

'Oh, sorry – er back there,' I said, pointing in the direction from which we had just come.

'You passed it then. It's ways back there over the hill.'

'Oh, we must have missed the sign.'

'I hope not,' she snapped. 'We don't want no damned signs around here – encouraging them watchers.' She paused and withdrew the nozzle from the car. 'Ya say you're from England?'

The tank was full.

'From Kent,' I replied.

'Oh, I've got a sister-in-law in England. Can't make head or tail of her letters. Can't read her writing. I even try writin' like her to get the sense of it or see if I can find out how she wrote. Damned if I can understand a durned thang! That'll be six dollars and twenty-seven cents.' I gave her seven dollars and waived the change.

'Give it to a doggy fund,' I said.

'I'll go one better. I have a crippled children box, I'll put it in there.'

We turned around and drove off. Then I stopped just around the bend, took out my notebook and made a small sketch to remember her by.

We then turned back again and drove past the garage and photographed it. It seemed such a shame to miss any details. And her with the face of a reptile – or a turkey vulture!

We took the road back the way we had come and tried to locate the elusive observation post. We were just giving up on our hunt for the condor, sick at heart, when I stopped to get another breather and take a look at a dead tree in the rolling landscape. There were two black shapes in the branches but they didn't look large enough to be anything but crows. I reached for my camera and decided to fit a telescopic lens. The shapes *were* crows but had flown off by the time I was ready to photograph them. I was getting back into the car when Anna pointed to a shape coming up low over the Tecuya ridge. It was massive, its flight pattern was slow and it hardly moved its wings.

It couldn't have been anything but a condor. This was majesty – and it thrilled the heart to watch it. The dihedral angle of its wings is almost flat and the bird's stability is aided by an upturned spread of black feathers radiating in singles from the tip of the wings, like fingers. Several times I managed to focus the

telescopic lens on the creature and press the shutter release. But there were as many times, if not more, I did not, as I was absorbed in watching this princess amongst birds. It was the crown to our journey, and even Sadie who before had been muttering, 'You and your vultures, Dad,' watched the sight with quiet interest and was impressed. She realised the search was over by concluding, 'Right! Now perhaps we can get back to LA!'

The Sheep of Maidstone

It is no accident that sheep have entered my life at last. I was brought up in a sheep farming town, but at the time showed no interest in sheep whatsoever except perhaps as being something to prod on my way home after school. I was not unusually cruel. All boys are like that, and I used to think that all sheep were for prodding. But I believe now that I was wrong about the sheep, and that boys are for prodding.

We are all God's creatures after all and the sheep of Maidstone (my local town) are living testament to the confusion we suffer. Why? he bleated. Because they do not possess self-knowledge. They do not know what is in store for them and they are, like so many of us, bereft of reason and sense; nevertheless, unlike us, they are stoic in their acceptance of life.

The Stoics believe that supreme good manifests itself in conformity to nature and its universal laws. They make virtue nearly synonymous with intelligence, and vice with error.

The founder of this school and the most famous Stoic in antiquity was Zeno. I gave this name to my head sheep. When Zeno and I confront each other in the orchard, everything becomes clear.

Zeno displays a dignity and pride given to but few women and even fewer men (feminist typist!). I seek him out daily and whilst he never confronts me head on he adopts a posture as though he has something to say. Life's wordless explanation is expressed in Zeno's eye. He shares with me his feeling of assured wisdom.

Zeno's pupil is square, as are all sheep's, and depending on his mood and demeanour the pupil will increase or diminish in size. It becomes a thin fine line when he is displeased and contemptuous. He will always show his feelings – such is his basic honesty. It is a quality I look for in people, but seldom find. Zeno also has the ability to make one think, and right now I have much to think about.

The difference between us, apart from the wool, is that I will exercise my will in favour of what I believe to be right and he will exercise his legs in an instinctive reaction against my attempt to get close enough to stroke his head.

And is there not wisdom in that? Old wisdom, and old stupidity too. But that's OK. Beware the new morality, that's all. Trust no one at present. They do not possess self-knowledge. It is the lambing season and the ram will come again.

Apart from the goat, the sheep is man's oldest domesticated animal. Zeno is so smart that in the few months I have known him he has learned man's vocabulary of honour, or was it passed on by his mother? Was his innocent wisdom a front until he had discovered my motives?

'Have you got one of these in your book?' It was a small orange rubber ring, like a mint with a hole. The farmer was holding it.

'What is it?' I said.

'They take the goolies off with it.'

'Bit small, isn't it?'

'They shoot them on with a stretch gun. You ought to see Mick when he only gets one ball in. Rips the ring right off again, with his fingers – right over the ball. Now, that really hurts!'

It might also account for the square pupil in Zeno's eye.

'Hi, Zeno, come here, why are you standing alone?' All the other sheep had rushed forward at the first sight of my mechanical hedge-clipper, for their daily disappointment. No food again! The bugger keeps bringing us no food, just bits of machinery and no food.

'Got you a cabbage,' I said, ignoring the baaing of the crowd and producing a home-grown beauty from behind my back.

Zeno still didn't move.

'Come on, Zeno, have some cabbage. Why so dumb?'

He turned his head sideways and his big left eye spoke a universe.

'Something on your mind?' I said.

. . . . . You said you'd save me. Am I really for the chop? I trusted you . . . . .

'Well I tried, Zeno – God knows how I tried. Farmers are funny people to deal with. I'm not sure – maybe you are saved. I'm not promising, but it is possible. I told the farmer I wanted to keep you . . .

'The farmer looked at me as though I had just mouthed a heresy. He said, "You don't *keep* sheep. You either butcher them or you breed them."

'He is a kind man though. He told me he would leave you here, but he would have to leave a mate too.

Mr Buckwell's flock and Zeno.

There are not many farmers who would say that – he said you could have that one over there. I know, she's ugly, but beggars can't be choosers. What do you mean she's your Mother-in Law? He's a nice sheep, look at that forelock – or is it a dreadlock? Look out! He's going for you. He fancies you. What did I tell you? You stick with me, Zeno, I'll see you all right. You look a bit flabbergasted, old sport. Say something, Zeno, your eye's gone dead.'

I didn't see Zeno for a week.

The Mother-in-Law.

Zeno-Sage, Stoic

114 Ralph Steadman

When I saw Zeno again he was driving his head into the side of one of his flock in a most aggressive manner, trying to corner the feed trough for himself. Was this the same civilised creature I had come to love and respect for his detachment, objectivity and wisdom? It was, and his current behaviour was something of a shock and a revelation.

I tried to grab his woolly back but he was quicker than me, and nipped around the trough to begin shoving again on the other side, driving his hard head between the bodies of his friends like a plough blade.

In those few moments, my rosy vision of him was shot to hell and so it should be – now we could discuss things man-to-man and Zeno would not have to live up to my unreasonable expectations. No wonder he looked sheepish when he emerged from the trough. All dinner parties are like that.

'I saved you from the butcher, Zeno, and now I have to feed you. Not just you, but your two pals as well. I had to buy Mother-in-Law, you know that. Then the farmer told me you were both useless. Clean bowled. So he sold me this little female. Thought you'd like that, Zeno! Don't push . . . you push more than the others. You're bigger too. And you're not as smart as I thought. The farmer tells me that the day he took the flock to market he had a job to separate you and your pals from the rest. You were always first, Zeno – out in front – into the truck – straight to the bucket. Head down before the others could get a look in. That was dumb, Zeno. I nearly changed my mind and let you go the first time you did that. In fact, the only thing that saved you was the flat tyre.'

. . . . . Flat tyre? . . . . .

I had Zeno's attention at last. He stopped tearing at the calabrese stalk I was holding and raised his big eyes. His left eye was looking straight at me. The eye that had separated him from the rest of the herd in the first place. His pals were still pulling at the calabrese.

'Yes! The farmer enticed all the flock into the truck. Then he tried to pull you out by the scruff of the neck. You resented that and struggled like an enraged bull. During the struggle a tyre went down. He was cursing bitterly and your name was mentioned a few times. He had missed the market by now. You were lucky. The flock had a week's reprieve.'

. . . . . You wouldn't *really* have let me go . . . . . His left eye was now throbbing with helpless appeal.

'Don't push your luck. Get greedy on me and you're off. And the bigger you get, the more money I'll make out of you. Got the picture? Sod's law. OK?'

His pals were still tearing at the stalk, now a mere pulverised stump. 'Tell your pals too,' I said pitilessly. Zeno nuzzled my hand and I melted instantly.

MONEY MONEY money

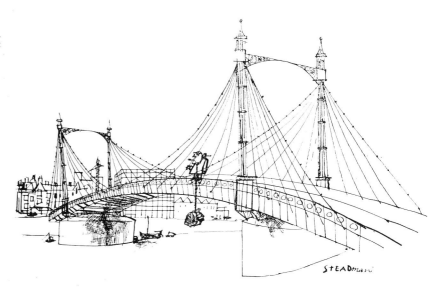

Money is a joy to behold and a thing for ever.

Money, as we all know, is currency. Currency is a medium of exchange in one form or another which exists in every community to facilitate the simple principle of barter.

I had just received a crippling bill.

Barter was the original form of exchange where commodities were offered in exchange for other commodities of a like value.

I wish we still used barter.

Problems arose with this method when the exchange of some commodities, otherwise desirable, would be effected with difficulty or prevented by the inconvenience of transportation.

So, in the natural exercise of transaction some goods would be in much demand by the nature of their individual qualities whilst other commodities would languish in their awkwardness and create hardship for their holders.

An excess of commodities with desirable qualities creates an unnatural glut in the market-place, outstripping demand and causing hardship for their holders but serving them right.

I walked towards the orchard musing on this.

A kind of currency developed from constant demands based mainly on the primary needs such as food and clothing: the staples of life. Corn and cattle were staples – the former was bartered amongst near neighbours, the latter had a more widespread market owing to its ability to move itself. In fact, many items came to be valued in terms of cattle, horses and *sheep*.

In the orchard the sheep had their heads down, picking desperately

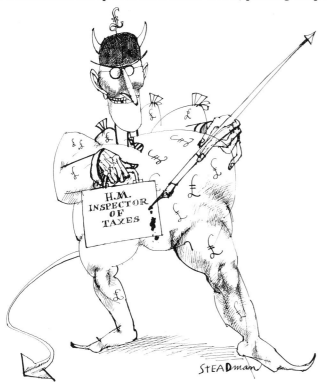

at the few remaining uneaten blades of grass. It's time *they* were bartered, I thought. Zeno wasn't eating, he was looking at me hard. He caught my eye and I felt compelled to speak.

'Ah, Zeno, you are not like the others, but in the market-place they couldn't know that. A sheep is just a sheep in a man's world. How much you weigh is the only thing of interest, with or without your balls. You are meat, Zeno, but not to me.'

. . . . . I know, small comfort. It's just that transactions have become more complex and refined. Difficulties arose with regard to visibility and change. To be owed half a leg of sheep is a difficult thing to resolve at the moment of transaction unless you could immediately find a third party who desperately wanted a sheep with three and a half legs . . . . .

Hmm, this sheep's smarter than I thought.

'So trade became limited,' I said.

. . . . .And the supply depended on a combination of conditions created by the joint operation of human industry and natural causes, which are so uncertain. Exchanges were perpetually hindered and subject to pure chance. Industry was either disturbed by successes which had not been merited, or disasters which were not anticipated . . . . .

'Yes, Zeno, it was finally realised that no quality was more desirable than steadiness of value and a constant relation between supply and demand. *Basic economics!* That's why sheep are still only sheep. Articles of common consumption lack this steadiness. It was realised with increasing glee that articles (including luxuries) which were not absolute necessities had this quality of steadiness.

'Metals particularly had this constant value.' I was warming to the subject. 'And, more importantly, those which became known as precious metals.'

. . . . . Ornament and show are fundamental to human nature, I've noticed . . . . .

'Yes! Those metals that lent themselves to the making of such ornaments and decoration became precious metals. Particularly gold, the colour of the sun, the giver of life. Your life, Zeno.'

. . . . . But I thought *you* had that power . . . . .

115

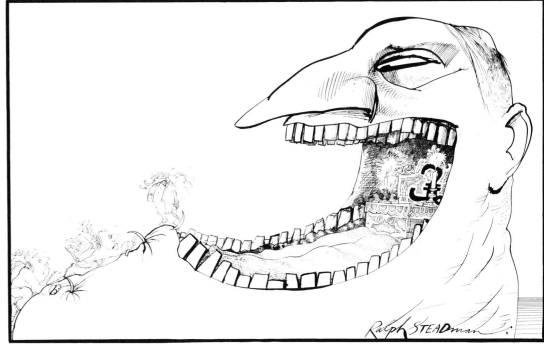

'In a manner of speaking, yes. Where was I? Gold – yes, gold!

'The demand for gold, however, is universally inferior to the demands for absolute necessities in times of famine and is therefore controllable and remains independent of such disasters. In times of abundance, gold is freely used as a luxury and maintains the demand and stability in the market-place. It was only by degree and after long experience that these qualities came to be realised as forming a true basis of a currency.'

. . . . . I see. You seem to understand the theory, but what you might not understand is government interference. Government interference more than any other single factor is responsible for giving your world a practical demonstration of greed, avarice and a hunger for power through the acquisition of this universal currency. If it wasn't for the banks, governments would be even more powerful than they are today. Ultimately it is the banks who hold the power, for it is they who invented themselves and their own sophistication. . . . .

'But not only that, Zeno, unfortunately, it is the banks who, because of the way they have also invented their own indispensability, have grafted themselves on to society and by doing so shaped our morals.'

. . . . . Some of you would object to that. Some of you actually *believe* that your morals are based on finer thoughts and not on money. Maybe they are, but money perverts them and money is your common desire. The banks are your blood supply, at the very heart of your society. They can also apply the tourniquet. . . . .

'You can say that again, Zeno, and in the event of revolution the jugular is cut and the body dies.'

. . . . .Yes, banks use the same method of control as the farmer used on my balls. If your morals are not warped by such persuasive methods it must be because you are too familiar with the process. The banks have become your life-support system, and therefore the arbiters of moral procedure. . . . .

'So that's why bank managers are looked upon as the most respectable members of society, next to vicars.'

. . . . . If you say so . . . . . Zeno turned away and carried on eating.

VIOLENCE as COMMON as MUCK

I mean violence in its broadest sense, not just a smack in the mouth but the violence of change. The violence in thoughtless behaviour. The violence in quick movement and the violence of noise.

Violence occurs in more ways than one when a row of old homes is requisitioned and demolished. A way of life is destroyed, a pattern of long-cherished habits sacrificed. A spirit of community and a sense of belonging are swept away and with it a complex embroidery of human input, happiness and tragedy. A history of slow growing – a richer passing of time.

We would do well to ask what we can add to that before we decide to sweep it clear and start again. If we obliterate the reference points completely we are in danger of substituting banality and brutality. The violence of bureaucratic decision is at work and the damage is

119

measurable only when it is too late. Too late for the shame and the pity and certainly too late for the platitudes of local councillors.

Architects are credited with the knowledge, taste and wit to guide such groups of people who make the decisions – the elected butchers, bakers and guildsmen of council halls – who wouldn't know a brick from a savage attack of constipation, let alone be capable of making plans for town development schemes which affect us all fundamentally. These amateurs have to employ a lackey to draw up the official, unstoppable fact of it.

I accuse architects of gross misconduct and violent acts against real people. Plans which turn people into units and place them in co-ordinated sections on paper are a denial of life and in that area, efficiency must take second place. Being an architect is not a career, any more than being a satirist or a doctor. Architects should be dreamers not administrators wielding the unquestioned powers of those who seem to know better.

The sanctity of life is paramount. The brutal pursuit of an idea for experimental reasons is a crime against humanity. I warn you that if you merely pursue an ambition to set up a lucrative practice on the backs of those who need a roof over their heads, this will bring nothing but misery where you could bring joy. Fight the economists. Everything you dream of can be achieved. People will respond to the natural aesthetics of life and prove your point. Where did the notion come from that a pleasant place to live must naturally cost more? Only from the economists and the scum of real estate.

Our world is freely given and beautiful. A present from the natural order. Give it room to breathe and restore to us all the heritage we know is there, as surely as we hold our begging bowls.

120

⑧ Der Könner   Ralph STEADman

① Der Normale   Ralph STEADman 76

⑥ Der Kämpfer   Ralph STEADman 76

⑦ Der Pflichtbewusste   Ralph STEADman 76

⑤ Der Skeptiker   Ralph STEADman 76

Gardening Hint No. 40

Glass is sharp and glass is clear and glass means light. Glass keeps in warmth and glass is great for looking out of. Newcastle Brown tastes best out of glass and so do whisky and gin. Adverts look best when glass is gleaming and displaying shattered ice. Glass is returnable. Glass is super to break when there's a fire and glass is something secure between you and the passing landscape outside a train. Sandwiches look better behind glass and so do pork pies and pictures.

Glass is there one moment and smashed the next. I wanted glass for my greenhouse of course. I was after a sort of crystal palace of a place and I was made the offer of a Victorian job of no mean proportions. A monster phantasmagoria of cast ornamental gussets and pillars. To get it up first was my intent and the only question I asked myself was: 'Will it fit?' My garden is not big by some standards and is walled all around. The growing season was at an end and I hankered after a new era of something tropical, exotic and demanding. A whole environment where a soul can lose himself for days on end

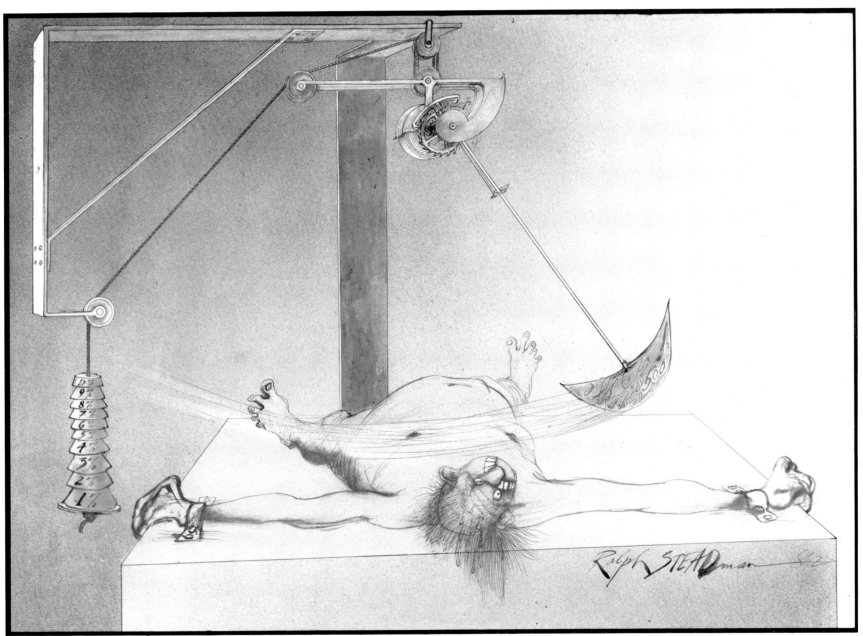

123

without coming home for tea. A place where each trip into the undergrowth is an exploration to another world, a steamy tramp up the Amazon and an encounter with lost tribes, heroic fights with vast hordes of soldier ants.

When thoughts like these invade the mind troublesome neighbours become snakes in the grass or loathsome creepy-crawlies. Local authorities turn into sabre-toothed tigers and the police draw on the dark mantle of panthers with yellow eyes stalking the undergrowth.

The crystal palace fitted over my garden perfectly. Within this formidable framework, monstrous examples of jungle vegetation were brought under control with root pruning based on the principles used by the Japanese to dwarf bonsai trees. Planned expeditions into the darkest undergrowth now became a weekly habit. I survived on K rations which kept me fit enough to ward off the attacks of Black Mambas and tsetse flies.

I am now seeing the results of my months of careful work. I give you an instance. A Plethora Maximumus whose daily diet included pythons, chimpanzees and cheetahs was just the thing, I thought, to top-graft with my neighbour's pure white dog daisies, thus tempering its appetite to reasonable proportions. If my hunch was correct this organism would devour my other neighbour's basset-hounds and an endless supply of alley cats which had laid waste many of my earlier horticultural experiments.

My work has been one hundred per cent successful and I am developing a similar Plethora Maximumus crossed with an Aspidistra which I stole from the Hammersmith Town Planning Department, to take care of any nosy council official who may have had complaints about lost pets.

And the gardening hint to potential Plethora Maximumus devotees is to handle only with heavy-duty mechanical tweezers, leather gloves, asbestos boilersuits and bull whips.

Graft on.

Next time: Petals are tougher than you think.

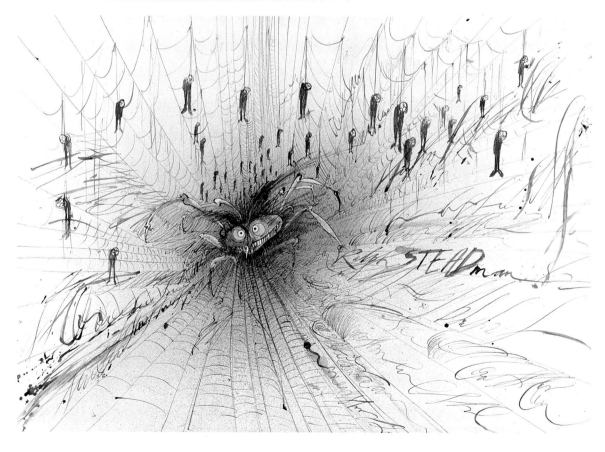

The appetites of – er – sexual life vary from person to person, indeed, from moment to moment. It's a sad fact that when people start writing about sex they are usually not getting any so I'll keep this short.

Gardening Hint No. 6

How was your asparagus? Gardening Hint No. 6 should deal with the last mowing of the lawn, but I don't see why I should tell you that you should disturb the grass roots with a spring-toothed rake first and aerate the surface of the soil with a fork, particularly in areas where moss is forming, because I haven't got a lawn. And if you don't disperse mole hills and worm casts as they appear, then you don't deserve to have a lawn either. I often find that the bigger the lawn the more selfish the people who own it. Some of the nicest people I know are small-lawn owners, but surprisingly some of my best friends are big-lawn owners. If gardening has taught me anything at all, it is simply to really get to know people and not just look at their lawns.

The more you get, the more you want and the funny thing is – the less you get, the less you get and the less you can get it. What?

A man in the middle of the Gobi Desert, or a woman for that matter (though fewer women than men stand in the middle of the Gobi Desert), may be burning with desire, but what for? What good is dry sand, eh?

Quite right, unless they can find each other in such a big place, their appetites will be diminished and will be replaced with a desire to get out of the hot sun. Unless they can find a camel – or a small tree stump. I suppose a small cactus would do, or a banana, but it is an old North African myth that there are bananas in the desert. There are not many cacti either, but as I was saying, there are probably not as many women as camels.

Therefore I think it is safe to say that sex in the Gobi Desert is down to a minimum unless you include the insects and the snakes. Snakes, in fact, have a hell of a time staying on and therefore manage coitus once every fifteen years, which is how long it takes for a snake to cross the Gobi Desert and find another snake in the first place.

As for insects, did you know that scarab beetles are all males who live alone for most of the time and only come together to mate, though no one has ever seen them at it, but when they do come together after these long, lonely absences, they always bring ten more scarabs with them and so they multiply. The legend has it that the scarab beetle mates with the sand and the sand gives birth, which is why the scarab beetle is a god in Egyptian folklore.

But a man in the middle of the Gobi Desert is no god at all. He's probably no good at all either. Rather a pathetic sight actually, unless he has been spotted by a woman who is also standing in the middle of the Gobi Desert, or at least near enough to the middle to see him. She could sneak up behind him, reach out and say 'Gotcha', and for a moment the man would be speechless with shock, but then he would

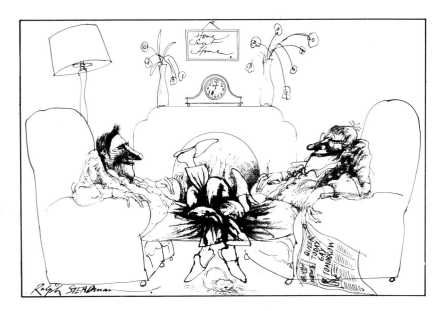

act like a god. Any port in a storm. Unless he hadn't had food and water, for nothing diminishes a hunger of desire like a lack of food and water. It dries everything up.

Well, he might just manage it once with a bit of help but his mind wouldn't be on it and if there's one thing a man has to do it's concentrate and even if she let him and he managed it, they would both be exhausted afterwards because of too much sun, because of no food and water and because of the other. And there they would be, lying down. They would hardly be standing up, especially afterwards – and the vultures would circle. Round and round above their heads, getting lower and lower, nearer and nearer, like they do.

And the most extraordinary fact of all is that there are only female vultures. How can this be? How do they have children? Well, I'll tell you. It is no accident that the vulture is the mother figure, Mut, goddess of fertility and high priestess of Egyptian mythology. . . The female vulture rises to a great height, then zooms off at speed in a cold downdraught. With a sudden jerking movement she is on her back and moving in the opposite direction with her legs wide open, at which moment she is mysteriously impregnated by the wind.

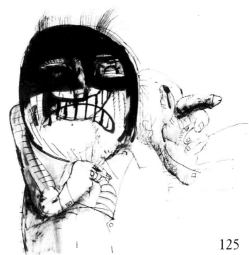

FACT

Did you know that according to the laws of England, if one or other party to a contract is completely drunk during the signing of that contract it renders the contract invalid?

So if you were drunk when you got married – you're not.

125

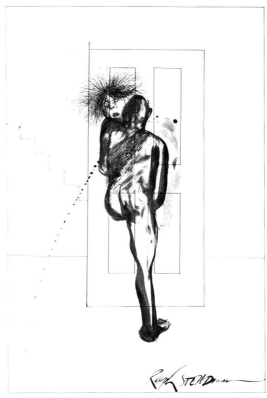
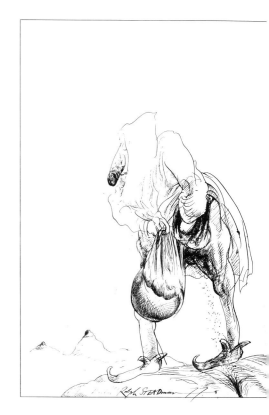

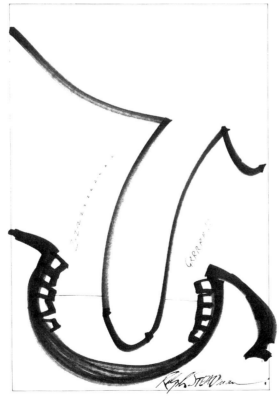

I did some drawings which appeared in *Gay News* some years ago to accompany articles about the difficulties homosexuals are confronted with in an alien society. The drawings make no comment whatsoever on those difficulties, but serve only to deflect and lighten the tone of the articles which, as I recall, were good and serious. However, I was interviewed by the paper at the same time, though as far as I know my comments were never published. This was possibly due to some criticism I made regarding an overt editorial preoccupation with the purely sexual aspects of gay life indulged in by that and most other gay magazines.

I suggested that this might account for the unfair and stony response all gays are victims of from a public already sexually inhibited by less complicated relationships. The natural reaction from people, and particularly anxious parents, would be to shun such periodicals completely, and therefore deny any useful dialogue likely to promote greater understanding and harmony on all sides.

I realise great inroads have been made since I offered such comments and gay rights have come on some, yet still have a long way to go to achieve an integration not known since the Renaissance.

Gardening Hint No. 21

'Oh pooh to you, I've got one!' This was no idle comment about the merits of one manure against another. This was a gentle, nice old lady clutching a Monstera Deliciosa to her bosom (which is why I noticed) and brandishing an airline ticket in the face of an airline official. 'No flight?' she gasped. 'But I paid for my ticket. I have a right to a flight!' 'No one, ma'am, has a right to a flight. That's why we're here, ma'am, to help you, ma'am!'

The Monstera Deliciosa she was holding quivered and began to act strangely. In an airport lounge strange things often do happen. Your sandwich starts talking, you begin to think that Lufthansa LH 504 to Hamburg is some kind of drink, flight numbers make patterns and don't add up, you think you've just watched Rod Stewart walk past Gate 16 to Brussels drinking milk, followed by six male hat stands chanting, 'Six things come to mind.'

Anyway, this poor lady, and that poor plant, trying to look away as only a plant can; I thought I was about to witness one of those suspended horrors where everything happens in slow-motion. And, of course, I was. The lady wilted, sure, why not? Anybody would under such pressure, and notice that while we are on the subject, officials always go for old ladies first. They leave unpleasant-looking sods like me alone until it is absolutely necessary. But that plant, my God! Suddenly and without warning the plant did what I always hoped a plant would do some day. It savaged an official. Not in the usual way, mind, you know, by

slapping him across the face with its largest leaf. The plant just leapt – yes, leapt – out of its paper wrapper labelled *Avis Ford Florist* and sank its teeth (I never knew a Monstera had teeth until then) into the official's well-padded thigh, padded, that is, with forms to fill in. The roots tore themselves from *John Innes Compound Number Two with Added Nutrient* and grasped the flailing arms, growing by the second. I never saw such roots! Whatever the official tried to do the plant had an aerial root to answer the question. The official screamed in sequence: 'Name: Arrghh! Address: Urarghugh! Sex: Eeeehahoooeeeh! Nature of business: Burrghurghel!'

Codiænum Variegatum Pictum, Aglaonema Commutatem, and several species of *Hedera* joined in the carnival, reminiscent of Jewison's film Rollerball, based on a short story by William Harrison.

The Monstera, meanwhile, struck out through Gate 6 for Mozambique. I followed, fascinated and protected by my *Friends of the Earth Gardeners' Badge of Merit*. Plunging through the electronic what's-its-name which registered absolutely nothing, and why should it, for the plant had nothing to hide, and taking the nice old lady with it, gently cradled in a new leaf, though why it should think she was making for Mozambique I can't imagine . . . But in situations like this plants don't think, they just grow. And its roots were far too deep now to stop and doubt.

Plants get a 'rush' just like people and bums.

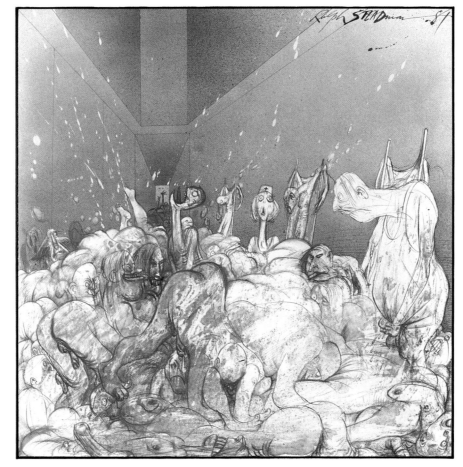

Thrusting its entangled greenery through the fuselage door, lady and all, the Monstera immediately filled the first-class area of the 747, bar deck and the pilot's cabin, totally taking over the controls, co-pilot and all. I was thrown into a seat six rows back in the economy section. Air hostesses and stewards reacted instinctively, for by now its phenomenal growing record had left its roots gasping for fertiliser. Rushing forward with the drinks trolley, a pretty red-headed hostess (Hi! I'm Cheryl! Fly me!) produced a large earthenware pot, a bag of John Innes Number Three Compost a few stones and a bucket of ice cubes (duty free).

She placed the few stones at the bottom of the pot, washing them over with a tin of iced soda water. She followed this with a few handfuls of John Innes and one handful of Bio-Humus. With some difficulty she grabbed and stroked the main roots, by now pulsing desperately, and caressed them into the pot, curling them around the edges as she went. The Monstera sobbed convulsively as reaction set in and it succumbed to the new soporific atmosphere of superlative service like a baby to a mother's tit. A pole from a gate barrier was produced and sunk gently into the compost beside the plant, now hiccuping sobs at longer intervals.

131

The old lady settled herself snugly inside a window seatbelt and called for a large gin and felt for the .45 secreted in her girdle. The plant was now at rest but still unable to absorb the goodness around the soil. With the consistent understanding for which air hostesses are famous the girl emptied a whole tin of American dry ginger over the soil's surface, binding root to matter. This was followed by the buckets of ice, laid evenly around all stems and protrusions.

The plant will now survive, provided it does not come face to face with a disembarkation card or such, though it will probably need watering with ice cubes at monthly intervals with a shot of soda or ginger ale. Plants develop likings and habits for things too, and why shouldn't they? They're only human.

Next time: One man's sunflower is another man's shadow.

Rooting for you.

St. Pauli — The Truck drivers rest.

132

Visit to a Victorian Caricaturist

Based on an article by W.P.W. Benson in the *Sheffield Portrait Gallery*, a journal of literature, criticism and satire, November 1875.

R. Steadman *after* J. Gillray

Edward Pitt Heath

until I find myself in a sort of cucumber frame right at the top of the house. Here I have to wait until I am half suffocated by the fumes of the patent inks and potions used in the manipulative art. Around me I see hundreds of grimy chimneys pouring forth dense volumes of smoke; and the sooty smuts flying about find a lodgment on the glass roof and settle down, blocking out the light, so that the sun can with difficulty be seen by the naked eye.

I stare savagely at several sitters until my turn comes. (Oh, that I could forget the miseries I endured!) The caricaturist comes and mauls me about with his ink-stained fingers, and forces my neck into a wooden frame. Behind me is a background, consisting of a spiteful

It is enough to make me weep to think of the number of caricatures my friends have persisted in forcing upon me; weep, not because of their ugliness or their beauty; no! but weep to think that they must all have endured an amount of suffering which no human mortal can describe.

Never shall I forget the day of my own misery as long as I live. I must have my caricature done to oblige my friends.

I choose a fine day; don my best bib and tucker; rake out my hair; curl my whiskers; and make myself as pretty and amiable as possible.

I reach the studio at last, and wend my way up a long flight of stairs, little church with a sort of balcony in front. I place my hat on a chair before me, and lest I should faint under the operation, I seize a chair with one hand and hold my umbrella in the other; and thus I stand like some confounded donkey, or waxwork figure in the Baker Street Exhibition.

After the operator has hocussed and pocussed me about a great deal, he informs me all is ready. He bids me look cheerful and I screw up my mouth like some laughing hyena and try to put on one of my prettiest smiles as the operation begins. There I stand like an ass gazing on vacancy, a dim mist before my eyes and a tripod surmounted by a flat sheet upon which a fearful image appears. These few minutes are to me like so many years, and every act and thought of my past life rises up before me.

At last the picture is done. Surely my mouth is not as wide as that? My toes never stick out like that! Surely the caricaturist must be seized with a brainstorm!

Look at your album. (If you have not got one, you are a living wonder.) There you may see a sight that would stagger a Doctor of

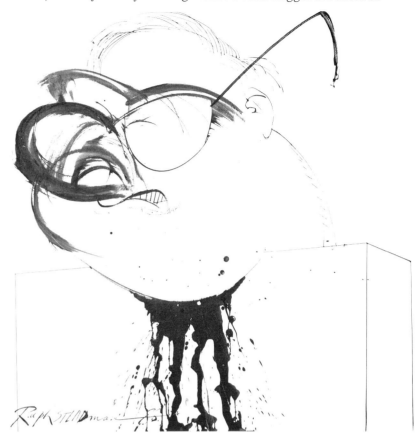

135

Divinity. You may yourself witness the torture your friends have undergone. One is grasping a table, another a chair; another has his legs crossed to prevent his knees knocking together; another holds his sides to prevent their splitting. Another digs his hands into his pockets to feel if he has money enough to pay for this abomination; and yet another gazes at some would-be warrior who seems as though he is about to send a spear into your breast. Show me one of your friends who looks comfortable. Show me one who does not look ridiculous. In every picture I see the wooden collar.

Why should I be pestered by everybody else's caricatures? Why should I spend a fortune to procure caricatures for everyone else? Why are we such slaves to fashion? Surely my friends are not so fond of me: they never used to take such interest! Cannot this fearful disease be cured? Tell your friends they don't look well to any caricaturist; they are too short, too long, too fat, too squat. The only perfect caricature I have ever encountered is 'The Perfect Cure', where the victim is seen dancing in mid-air.

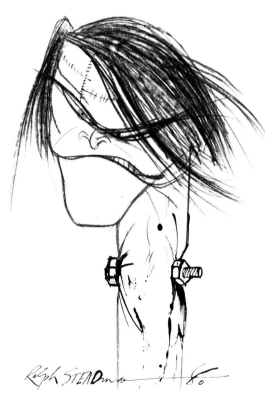

Gardening Hint No. 47

It was the small headlines I was beginning to notice, like AFTERSHAVE DRINKERS: NEW ADDICTION MENACE; WATER-DIVINER KNIGHTED; and FIRST CACTUS SEEN ON BED OF RIVER THAMES.

What had plagued the farmers of the prairies and the Great Plains in the 1930s had finally come to England. The dust-bowl menace. Dear old, lovely old, sweet old, lush-and-green old, friendly, faithful old England was becoming a dust bowl, with no rain forecast. At great expense, thirsty government officials are employing rainmakers and witch doctors, sages and gurus of all denominations to no avail. People drag their parched bodies from pub to pub hoping for the tiniest drop of warm flat beer slops left in the corner of an ashtray. Sweat is selling at £20 a fluid ounce. Dehydrated dementees from all walks of life suck on anything remotely damp.

To be a gardener at such a time is like being a Nazi as the Russians entered Berlin, and I keep my opinions about growing veg to myself, but being a gardener was never salad days anyway. It's a tough life. Soil conditions are never ever right: too wet, too dry, too acid, too alkaline, too rich, too sandy, too chalky, tomorrow and tomorrow and tomorrow.

Listen, when your back's against the garden wall, you make do, right? Our pioneering forefathers didn't consult their pocket green-thumb guide when confronted with a wasteland and the beating sun. Neither could they reach for the hosepipe. They dug a well before the latrine, planted beans and wept on them.

A happy gardener is a bad gardener. Gardening is a calling and sacrifices have to be made. The greatest gardeners have known deep sadness in their lives and weeping is a regular pastime which

138 *they share with their flowering*

Ralph STEADman

offspring. *Nothing is wasted and tears are a nurseryman's sundries. Well, a lot of them actually wallow in orgies of self-pity over the plight of their wilting orchids, usually because they lack the ability to grow them. But orchids demand genuine grief. Your average crocodile tears just won't wash. Orchids are not known as the flower of the mind for nothing. Don't imagine you can fool them for a moment with some maudlin drivel. Your heart must be open and vulnerable, bearing the experience of deeply felt sorrow.*

Orchid growing in Tahiti, strange to relate, has never been better since the influx of bloodless tourists with Gauguin-glazed eyes leaving venereal diseases, jukeboxes and Western appetites in their wake, and so Tahitians have made the most of the situation and channelled their grief. Grief is now their local industry in a packaged paradise.

How I got from London to Tahiti in a few rambling sentences I cannot imagine. It must be the thirst pangs drying out the cells of my brain and the ink from the typewriter ribbon I've been sucking on affecting my reason. My mind is wandering. But my garden is bursting with growth. I stand amongst it and cry out, 'My God, my God, why hast thou forsaken this green and pleasant land?' And my tears fall like morning dew on to the fertile planes of thrusting leaves or dribble tenderly down the tendrils of Pleione Formasana and its like, the terrestrial orchid from the mountains of Taiwan, and they too now weep for me.

May your compassions be aroused.
Next Time: Before the flood.

The top drawing on the left was done in the presence of the then very frail Sir Julian Huxley and I endeavoured to draw an extremely sympathetic portrait of him. Sadly, Lady Huxley, being naturally overprotective, objected most strongly to its use alongside an article about her husband to be published in the *Sunday Times*. Later I took the development a stage further and produced a far more severe version. This second drawing is in a strange way more faithful to the great man's strong underlying character, which shone through in spite of his physical frailty.

I never did find out which drawing Samuel Beckett preferred.

(with sort of huge apologies!)

Suffer little Children

When the 1960s got under way I felt pretty hopeful and even dared to imagine that each new drawing was a nail in the coffin of old values or rather old patterns of behaviour which were full of privilege and injustice. It's a strong feeling when you're young. You really believe things will change. So I worked with conviction. It genuinely felt like a cause. There was good and there was bad in the world and I was with the good. Knocking things down was meaningful fun. I didn't bother myself with what to put in its place. That wasn't my job. I was demolition. Though I worked for newspapers on a freelance basis, I felt the frustration of their editorial control and knew in my heart that I couldn't really believe in their motives. Some less than others. Every so often I'd turn my back on it all. I tried children's books. There's a world of jolly, bright colours, gentle fun and simple morals. Everything must turn out right and children must go to sleep with happy thoughts. One such story was *The Jelly Book*.

During the 1960s there were my own children pushing and growing. My second daughter Genevieve was two and a half when she developed a perforation of the stomach wall and required an operation. She was confined to Westminster Children's Hospital where she ultimately spent two months recovering. During that time Christmas came and went so I offered to decorate the walls of the ward and the things that impressed me most about children in hospital was the amount of jelly and ice-cream consumed. I shut out the sight of the vegetables in glass cases which were somebody else's children. At that time there was nothing in my vocabulary as an artist that could deal with that. Those are overwhelming odds. I always marked off in my brain a 'thank-you' for each healthy child. It's funny how things lie somewhere inside the mind, then one day due to circumstance, requests, independent development, drives and interest, they all converge and a way of coping with a subject emerges. I doubt if we will ever solve the problems of the Third World and by that I mean eradicating all poverty and hideous conditions from the face of the earth but with a little effort from everybody it might just be possible to save the children. We owe them that.

Before I was to draw my Save the Children pictures a lot had to happen. I went to America which caused the most fundamental change to take place so far.

Perhaps it was the break-up of my marriage in 1969 that caused me to look abroad or at least to look for a broad – Maggie Thatcher was an unknown junior minister then – and all the best obsessions are love affairs after all, so it wasn't that at this point. The island chauvinism of the English had finally got to me. National claustrophobia. It was time to go to the colonies. I chose America, and hopped out full of anticipation on a BOAC flight costing £104 return.

My love-hate relationship with America began when I met Hunter S. Thompson. He stimulated an inactive nerve in me. He exposed me to the screaming lifestyle of America. The raw violence. My drawing became stronger, less flaccid. He helped me to recognise my real targets – the Nixons of this world, the natural caricatures of life.

Caricature is still a game and at its best – as, for instance, during the Weimar Republic – a very dangerous one.

It's a sad fact that oppression, deceit, injustice, bestiality and violence are the mothers of satire. An unhappy person is a satirist without a cause, not because he applauds the darker side of life, but paradoxically because without that which he hates he feels redundant. And unhappily, he is rarely out of business, although some periods in history are more conducive to satire than others.

Many periods spring to mind in which satire had a vital role to play: among them: the early 1960s in England and America, when older values were dying on their feet; 1968 during the Sorbonne uprising which produced nothing in social terms but a marvellous short-lived journal called *L'enragé*; and the interminable Watergate affair of 1973.

Satire is companion to every side of human nature but whether it has any effect on the outcome of political and social situations remains doubtful.

Caricaturists and politicians and injustice are as perennial as the grass and although the caricaturists will never gain as much respect and attention as the politician, they are as necessary. Maybe far more necessary. Good satirists stand like sentinels till the day they die, and although it appears that they are no longer in operation, they never completely discard the self-inflicted burden they assumed to put the world to rights. They know in their hearts that they really can't, but persist even though some part of them craves a gentler outlook, to be a potter perhaps or a painter of lovely pictures or a teller of short stories.

They might even want to be entertainers or musicians or even shoesellers serving at people's feet, but somewhere at the back of their minds there's a mosquito called Methuselah. The bugger is indestructible.

Julie Omeally

INNER LONDON EDUCATION AUTHORITY

CHARLES LAMB PRIMARY SCHOOL

Popham Road, London N1 8RF

Headmistress Mrs. A. J. Jones   Telephone 01-226 2407

Dear Ralph Steadman
I Read Your book and
I found out you made
a mistake in the the
Jelly-book when I Read
it You Put "the Jelly-
Squasher who name
is Barry" you Shound
of Put "the Jelly-
Squasher who's name
is Barry". I Like Your
book's very much
I am 8 years old
wrote to m like if you

RALPH STEADMAN'S JELLY BOOK

DENNIS DOBSON LONDON

For Great Ormond Street and Westminster Children's Hospital

In a land where the sun shines all day long grow the jelly trees and each jelly tree is cared for by a friend.

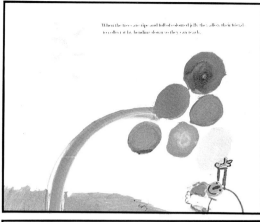

When the trees are ripe and full of coloured jelly they allow their friend to collect it by bending down so they can reach.

Off to the jelly factory goes the jelly by friendly elephant.

And . . .

Inside jelly inspectors sort out the good jelly from the bad. The bad is used to stuff pillows and mattresses.

GOOD JELLY

BAD JELLY

The good jelly is then taken across the lake in a jellyboat. It doesn't really have to go across the lake but everyone knows how much Good Captain Cyril likes to take the jelly for a sail so they don't really mind.

JELLY BOAT

It is then unloaded at the jetty by expert jelly unloaders.

When carried quickly to the jelly testers where pieces of each colour are tasted for flavour and quality.

It is now time to sort the jelly into its flavours and this is how it's done.

Jelly must be mixed up properly to make it smooth. Jelly mixers play a game to keep them happy at their work.

The jelly squasher whose name is Barry is a very strong man who can squash jelly into one hard lump.

To be cut up into smaller lumps and dropped into packets.

It never leaves you, that nagging urge to comment on society's bloody nonsense and its phoney moralising and pious indignation. That's *my* job – to moralise and to be piously indignant and since we live in an age of feverish demarcation and specialisation, why shouldn't I get bolshie about my little acre, and anyway I think I want to be a shepherd. 'Blessed are the meek.'

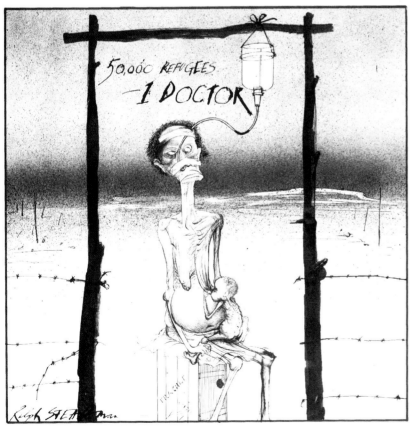

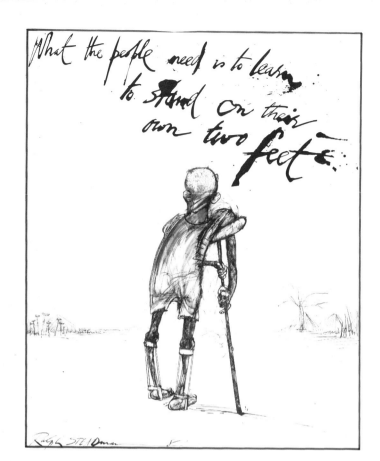

148

Darkest AFRICA

I caught a particularly virulent hot dog in Brussels airport. I called the airport authorities and God bless 'em, they shot it.

Announcer at Brussels airport whispers soft words of flight numbers to you like she's on the next pillow.

At Gate 6 my fellow passengers are lay preachers, missionaries, black professors, moustachioed 'Old Bills' and strange uncertain no-no's of extremely well fixed addresses.

As I enter the plane I breathe a last deep breath of fresh air and enter a stuffier clime. A disagreeable body odour lies heavy on my clothes and I don't think it's me (oh yes it is). Thank God for the refresher towel.

Where the fuck are we? On the way to blackness I think! Bugs everywhere – wherever I sit, so does a bug. We are now in Nigeria, which is part of Africa. Need a beer. Transit Bar – who needs

Nigerian money? The Transit Bar accepts a pound and gives me one-armed bandit discs in exchange. OK, so it's £1 for a beer. Let's get on.

5.30 am October 1974: Arrive.

Orange in the trees. Gentle ride from airport to Intercontinental Hotel across straight flat plains.

Africans – girls sauntering, baskets on heads – people wait for hundreds of yards along the mud sidewalk for something – they strobe the landscape – like an irregular pulse – I don't know why they wait and couldn't ask.

Dull, dawn sky – slight drizzle. Taxi is broken down but it works somehow.

Arrive at the Intercontinental Hotel telling the driver in crippled French that if he waits I'll change a Bank of America cheque and pay him. No room for me recorded. Somebody has fucked up again. I argue a little. Gentle and beyond reaction, I wait.

'Ralph! Goddammit – where you bin?'

Hunter – whisky with ice in one hand, credit card wallet in the other, sweating, early morning red eyes – weighs in heavy. My

Welcome to Kinshasa 05.30 HRS 24.10.74. EXIT

Ralph STEADman

naturally gentle English manner restrains him from pulling the head off the concierge.

'We can't change your travellers' cheque, monsieur, you don't have a room here.'

'Mais oui! I do! *Rolling Stone* – half a million sales in America alone – booked me in . . . assured me . . . guaranteed it!'

'Sorry sir.' Pause. He looks down and carries on writing. I insist again. He doesn't look up. I don't exist.

I just hit the strange lethargic NO that stops your adrenalin dead. You can stand in the same spot for any given length of time amidst any sort of conversation and just look at each other – him over there, you over here – immovable. And at 6 am on a Sunday morning nobody is going to shift. Not him and not me. I've had enough.

Hunter moves but he is already deep into something else; I have no possible inkling of what. I have just arrived. I go along.

I follow him out of the lobby carrying everything with me and stagger into an Avis car. The rain covers me like the fear that, at this moment, takes hold of my numbed brain.

Already, this is it? Not already! I'm innocent. Hunter has a friend with him, Bill Cordosa of the *New Times* masquerading as a *Rolling Stone* reporter. Stoned after six weeks of Zaire, heavy dope and no way home. Happy – sort of – but resigned and a tiny bit hopeless.

Hunter starts the engine with the car in gear, stalls, starts again, grinds on first – no, reverse – backs up – jerks forward, the drink in the left hand spilling, credit cards fluttering everywhere. Bill sways and snuggles up to Hunter involuntarily as the car tears away and out of the car lot. Bill sways again as Hunter misses a turn, swears, spills more drink. Does he really know what he's doing?

The car is in second all the way – engine revving – hot oily smell. Car is on fire. Or should be. Six blocks one way, three another, half a turn this way, two double backs, four wrong turns. We arrive in flames. The club is on the corner.

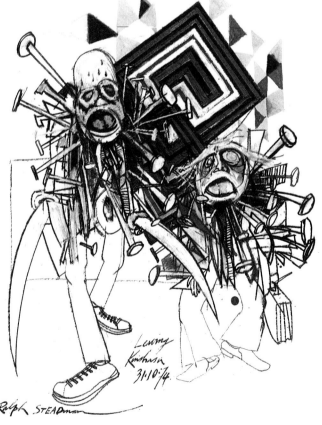

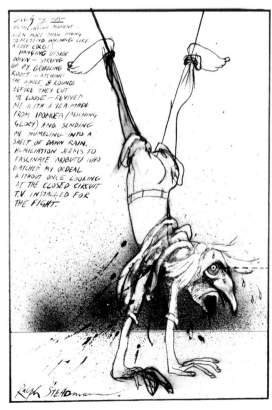

(Remember it's 6 am.) Bill disappears. We look for him in a dirty early morning room.

No one but a man finishing the dregs of every glass in the place and us looking about, lost. Up for grabs almost.

'Where's Bill?' Hunter asks.

Why Bill, I wonder. We just had Bill in the car.

'What we doing here?' I say aloud.

'Look for Bill,' Hunter snaps.

Why? Who's Bill – see him – two blocks away – hunched – droopy – unsteady – walking home in the wrong direction to the Memling Hotel. Follow him in the car – how many blocks – try three – we practically run him down –

'Hi! Hi man! I'm just going home – gotta sleep.'

'Steadman needs a room.'

'Be my guest!'

'Just one moment,' say I. 'Where are we, why and who – OK, never mind – thanks anyway.'

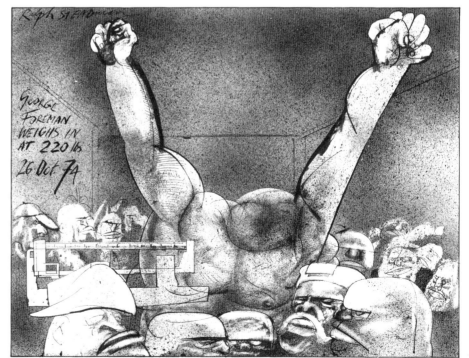

153

Hunter and me in Zaire – a small incident

I was describing a small incident that happened in Zaire to Bill Murray, the actor playing Hunter.

'We were in Kinshasa covering the Ali–Foreman fight for *R.S.* We spent a lot of time around the pool. One afternoon a light airplane flew over pulling a banner which bore the words "Mobutu Welcomes You to Kinshasa".

'"Oh God," said Hunter and he has this kind of half smile, held back, and a faraway look in his eyes as though he's thinking ahead and he probably is. "I'd like to hire that fucker up there for an afternoon," he said. "Oh yes, we could write a screamer for that ourselves, Ralph, with those big pens of yours. Something to really send shock waves through the nerve ends of everyone here. Something like – " and he's looking down like this – through the floor, as it were – "something like 'Black is Weird!'".

'Don't forget the feints and nods with the head – his head jerks back when he lights a cigarette – like he's short-sighted and can't see the tip of it. Try it, like this!'

Everyone starts jerking their head back, and for a moment we are a roomful of chickens all strutting and clucking.

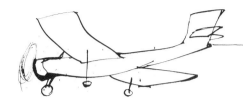

BLACK IS WEIRD

155

Poets are people

I live for poetry but poets do not live for me.

I wait for them to feed me like a starved rabbit. They do not know this.

It is better that they do not know how much they are needed. Otherwise we would be overcome by them, and they would not know when to stop.

A surfeit of poets would not be a good idea for our world. Our world needs only a certain number. Although that number may not have been reached, controlled poetry is important.

I know. I have watched poems hang about, waiting to pounce. It is worse than mugging. A horrible sight. An attacked person will run out into the street and shout. He may even curse the system, and leave home taking your daughter with him. Poems have a way of affecting the poor slobs who write them.

Poets remain silent during conversations, waiting for a lull. Suddenly, without warning, a poet will speak one sentence he has just thought of, and those around him will scream as though struck by an electric bolt.

Would you want that to happen too often? It could take months to return to anything resembling normality. It may be all right once in a while, for a change. But pause a moment and try to imagine Her Majesty's government broadcasting every day as they do, and every one of them a powerful poet.

The confusion would be indescribable. A nation would stop in its tracks and pick flowers for neighbours. Cars would jam in thick traffic and their drivers disgorge and shake hands. Strikes would be unnecessary for nobody would work. Life would be too good to miss. Each day would be lived without plan and each moment savoured like new wine. Each sunset would be a revelation and a promise for tomorrow.

Everybody would make love. Even the sick.

Better that poets should not use words. Better they were born dumb. Better that they cut their tongues out, should they speak. And better still if they think, they remain quiet. God protect us from their wild invocations until we have at least had time to practise a dead

poet's exercises, so that we are fit enough to try again today.

Poets do not realise. Whilst they live, they are weeds. When they die, they are fertiliser.

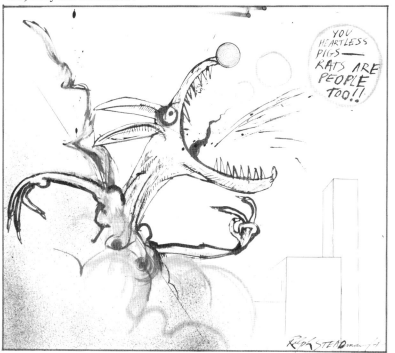

YOU HEARTLESS PIGS — RATS ARE PEOPLE TOO!!

Gardening Hint No. 45

Marcel Proust was never my idea of a perfect gardener. And neither were Genet and Colette, to drop a couple of names. Flaubert could have been; he was sensitive in a tender way. Émile Zola was too dry. Dusty cobwebs grew and covered his thoughts. Your fingers must quiver and throb with emerging buds. You must be fresh and vibrant. Optimistic. Given to dancing in the streets and raising the temperature of the coldest day. Damp with sweat and earthy tumescence. Think of a writer. Kerouac, Kesey, Ginsberg, Shaw, Wells, Wilde, Orwell, Auden, Isherwood, Faulkner, Miller and Durrell, Gilbert and Sullivan, Churchill and Hunter S. Thompson, even.

The names trip off my tongue easily

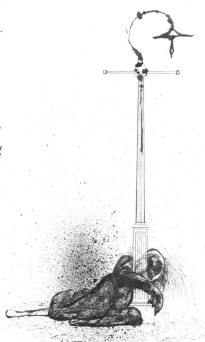

now, where before they choked what little confidence I had in my slight knowledge of them. Sure, they were fertiliser for the mind; rich, but not gardeners. None of them.

They oppressed my soul with all those words. Thousands of time-consuming words, hitting my resisting mind in solid blocks. Their contribution was substantial, but mute. The world went on the same and still goes. They remain a silent mass of sentinels, endlessly spelling the alphabet in the name of truth.

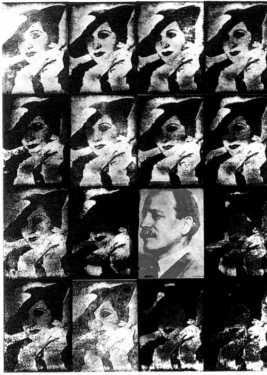

One day a plumbing engineer arrived to fit my central heating. To enable him to proceed it was imperative that my bookshelves be moved. All those books I had so religiously marshalled in rows had to be shifted for the plumber to fit his pipes. Without the pipes life could simply not go on. The pipes were important, indispensable. Of course, he was right. It was logical. Pipes flow with hot water necessary to provide warmth. Therefore to get from A to B you must have pipes, whatever the cost.

My living room collapsed into a heap of useless paper. So I threw it all into a dark corner of the garden without a qualm. It lay there in the rain and the changing climate. The thoughts and aspirations of the true fighters of guerrilla warfare lay damp and rotted away. I watched them go. I watched their pages curl and twist in agony and I smiled, happy in the knowledge that inside my house I was warm and secure. Centrally heated.

To cut a long story short, for decay takes time, I was eventually to learn that all these writers had a deep common bond. Fertiliser! Rich and wholesome. Even Mein Kampf.

When I dug this soggy mass of pulp into the good earth I was richly rewarded. When it comes to good fertiliser, the difference is the same. The diversity of ideas is the breeding ground of bacteria and the foundation for a good crop of vegetables.

Next time: Ten years on. What a long, strange thing is a bean.

157

A MATING RITUAL

*(Overheard on the Amtrack Metroliner
from Providence to New York)*

'I don't believe anything anybody
tells me. I don't believe nothing –
unless they gonna pay me!! I don't give
a flying fuck what anybody gets, but if
they pay me, OK. That's different.'

'Ya sure ya wanna help me? OK.
Then shurrup!'

By the time this couple gets back to
New York they'll be drunk beyond
their usual condition. Their
conversation reeks of animosity,
despair . . . I'll die if I feel like it,
punctuated by the odd angry expletive.

'Who the hell are you? You're
nuthin', you're nobody. I have a few
bucks, so what. I don't have to jump
for nobody. I don't care.'

Care is written into every puffy fold
of her corpulent frame. Her eyes
express a desperate disappointment.
Life's depressing.

'I don't wanna talk to people. I don't
care. Who the hell are you?'

Her companion wears a soft peak cap
over a Bowery boy face. He listens.
Whatever goes on between them – he is
wrong. He takes her flak. He answers
without her conviction.

'Skip it, you gonna cause a lotta
trouble. I don't wanna listen. I'm sick
of you.'

'I'm sick of you too.'

'That makes two of us.'

'I don't care.'

'You're drunk.'

'Let's drop it.'

'You're drunk too.'

'Matter of fact I'm leavin' when we
get back.'

'Yeah, that's what they all say, oh
boy. You sure are – .'

She takes a pill. Scratches her upper
lip just below the nose, rather
strangely. Her fingers move in a
deliberate emphatic way.

'Just shut up.'

A picture of misery on a train, as
though they took a ride to work things
out.

158   She continues. 'I know what you're

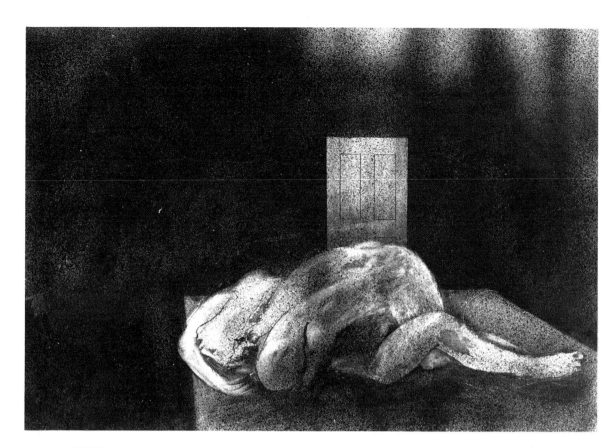

mad about. You just don't like people.'

'I don't dislike people. I take to certain people.'

'You don't give people a chance. You don't give people a chance. You're finished. Yes, finished.'

He seems to have a more optimistic manner. He speaks. 'Why don't you get off at Newark?'

'Pardon me?'

'Why don't you get off at Newark?'

'You're a fuckin' mystery . . . you know what I mean.'

'Why do you say that?'

'Because it's true – you're a misfit and I don't like to bother you with anything.'

'Are you trying to upset me?'

'You're a misfit.'

'Oh all right, shoot me.'

'I'm too drunk with mystery. I'd miss and waste a bullet, otherwise I would.'

She is silent again.

'You get a buck here, you get a buck there and you know what I mean. We are a couple of misfits, but you are burned out. At least I got common knowledge.'

'I think you should go back.'

'No, I never go back.'

'Hell, you are burned out to a crisp. You're fried to

159

a crisp. Your brain's gone.'

'There's no coming back to reality.'

'I don't want to go back.'

'Yeah let's go back together. Let's go back and be toast together.'

'Do you wanna 'nother drink?'

'Toast and freedom.'

'You know what you are. You're bombed out.'

'I don't wanna . . .'

'Shutup, so shutup.'

'You are bombed out.'

'You are so bombed out. You're toasted.'

'Shutup, shit, I wanna 'nother drink.'

'I don't travel with bugouts. I don't travel with bugouts.'

'I don't travel with bugouts, either.'

'You know what. I don't *like* bugouts.'

It goes quiet. I think they are looking at me.

Why does he write every time we talk?

'Sir. Sir! Can we have another drink? Another drink for the bugout. I'll have another Scotch. You'll take a fifty?'

'Hold on. I don't travel with bugouts. I'm going back to Long Island.'

'I wanna go back to Long Island too.'

'I don't travel with bugouts. I've put up with you long enough.'

'Oh shutup will you.'

'Who the hell are you?'

'I'm me. You are a bugout.'

'I don't give a flying fuck. Just shut up.'

'Why do I care, I don't have a care in the world.'

'Good luck to you . . .'

'That's 'cos you're a bugout. One life for you – on the street.'

She gives money for drinks – smiles for first time. Quiet again.

'Well – .'

Quiet.

'You bugout much better than me but that's beside the point.'

'You're a bugout and that's the point.'

'Put it up now or shut up.'

'Boy I'm glad I'm gettin' rid o' you.'

His voice is grating.

'I said all right but the dog don't go with you. The dog goes with me!'

'Huh!'

Soft hat, black T shirt, too short. Buttocks showing. Black jeans with white stitching. Listless. Unhappy.

'Just shut up.'

' – and shut up.'

'Bugout.'

'Bugout too.'

The man keeps looking over at me – curious.

Why do I keep writing? So she's curious because I keep writing even though the conversation has stopped again.

But that's the trick. Keep writing. Just avoid eyelock.

He thinks I'm writing it all down. He gives me sly looks. He has street sense. He knows.

A woman who has been studying a
map for one hour looks hard at him.
He really has a strange look. He is
younger than the girl – or she has
simply gone to seed on junk food.
    'What the what fuck one you are.'
    'Bullshit!'
    Silence.
    Nothing. Talked out. Tired.
    'OK shit face.'
    'Let's change stops.'
    It seems settled and I suspect that
what they do is part of a mating ritual.
    Dying spasms of conversation.
They have finally decided the
outcome.
    I don't wancha with 'im.
    I don't care.
    OK but don't blame – .
    I can jump fences all the time.
    I'll still rap all the way to the bank.
    I'm going to tell you the absolute
truth right now . . .
    Oh yeah?

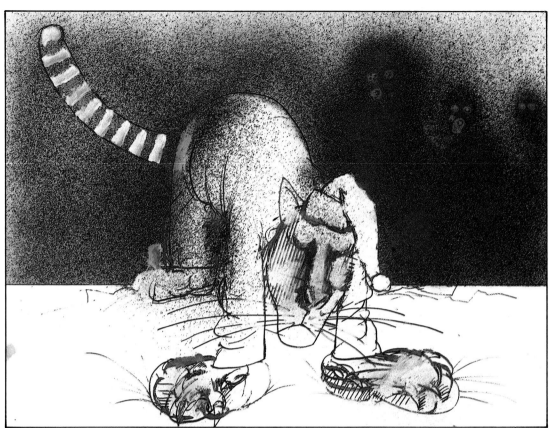

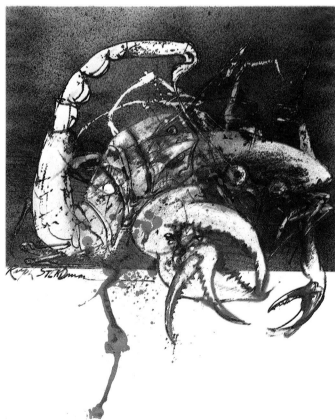

Charlie's Mum

We can maintain a Royal Family effortlessly, yet we still can't find a cure for the common cold.

Apart from that, I have absolutely nothing against them. The Queen is a real lady of the highest order and apart from one or two apparent hangers-on, she appears to need most of the people she gathers about her. God knows there are enough hangers-on in the most democratic walks of life, so it would be grossly unfair to single her out for special scrutiny.

She is at least a *real* Queen and that is the stuff of fairy tales and in fairy tales hangers-on get their come-uppance, so they don't hang on long, which probably means they are smarter than she is if they do, and deserve their position for as long as they can hold it. After that, hang 'em in Parliament Square. That is, after all, their code, otherwise they wouldn't suck up so enthusiastically to their chosen profession.

And if they ever get a common cold, hanging is the best cure for it. Nobody can have it both ways, not even the Queen. When she gets a cold, she doesn't just get a common one. Oh, boy! – she gets a special one, a real sonofabitch. But you never hear her complain, about that or anything else she might suffer from. She is probably in agony sometimes. That's the sign of a *real* Queen. You would never know.

The law may be an ass but its practitioners are devious and villainous scum who embrace the understandable problems of ordinary folk and render them incomprehensible and beyond their control.

When a problem is transformed into legal terms a human indiscretion becomes a heinous crime, and worse, written in a language known only to members of the legal profession, forged in antiquity and smugly endorsed by the infinite power of the Crown. What may have started as a simple dispute between two people becomes a faceless battleground where emotional response is stifled, only to re-emerge and manifest itself in mental and physical anguish upon the parties concerned.

Well, as far as I am concerned, that is not a service. But people get paid for that kind of work and that means something is wrong. The legal profession stinks of vested interest and a dark protection for the chosen few. Those honest enough to realise it should get out now, and get into politics, or something else equally worthless. At least they can crawl out of the woodwork honourably, but they should hurry.

The problem with the law is that you cannot legislate for a human impulse and a simple feeling and so, ultimately, the people most concerned get hurt badly. There's nowhere else to go for guidance but the law, the filthy, twisted law. And those bastards know it, and use it, and milk it.

Gardening Hint No. 28

'Life is a catacomb,' declares Professor Victor Demone, Ph.D. (Cantab) of Aldershot University.

Professor Demone has just spent the last decade studying the life of the common earthworm and its relevance to modern man. His findings are dynamic and likely to cause earth tremors wherever there is soil.

Professor Demone knew that the earthworm exhibits the essential annular characteristics – the body being segmented and the nervous system consisting of the typical ventral gangliated cord. Lateral appendages are wanting but they get by without them. They have a digestive system and a form of cerebral mechanism to think things out. They have eyes too but it is not certain even now quite why. Neither does the worm know. Nor does he use them as they remain closed twenty-four hours of the day, presumably to keep out the soil.

What is the use of all this information to the gardener? In fact, Professor Demone didn't discover anything vital about worms at all. But he did learn a lot about gardeners. He has stripped bare the strange behaviour of most of them and given us an insight into their perpetual mutterings as they dig and till and weed and sow. He himself donned a simulated rubber worm suit and burrowed his way through the topsoil of his laboratory garden, under the fence and into next door. His neighbour, a very keen and successful gardener, was picking his nose and transplanting tender young convolvuluses with which in recent years he had had significant success. When picking his nose again he proceeded to rearrange his thriving Lavatera into hedgelike rows. Professor Demone noticed that before attempting anything, whether it be overwintering chrysanthemum stools or mulching his prizewinning sweet peas, he always picked his nose. He never touched a single living organism without picking his nose. Professor Demone's conclusions were obvious. Gardeners, he thought to himself, have a nasty habit of picking their noses.

Burrowing on to next door but one, he found Mrs Pugh at No. 99 scratching her bottom thoughtfully before successfully layering several stalks of the rhododendron which carried off three firsts at last year's all-rhododendron championships.

Burrowing on yet again, Professor Demone happened upon the most amazing discovery to date. Leonard Borders, crown grafter extraordinary and gladioli whiz kid, was picking his nose and scratching his bottom furiously at the same time. His garden was a blaze of colour and it was still only March! The secret was out. Professor Demone had stumbled on the mystery of green fingers.

Next time: The truth about tomatoes. Fertilise a friend!

I really can't imagine why the Queen lends her support to such a profession. Doesn't she realise what they are like, or are her gentle hands tied by tradition? I think someone should have a quiet word in her ear, because there are a lot of lawyers about, and particularly at the functions she has to attend like the Lord Mayor's Banquet and the opening of Parliament.

You will always find them toadying at the seats of power, crawling around the rich and fawning upon the aristocracy, playing on the vanities of those hungry for flattery. And they are clever at it too. That is their gift; a way with words, and an appetite for human weakness.

Perhaps we should start phasing the profession out before we enter the twenty-first century, because it will take quite a while to brush away all those cobwebs and reveal to the people just how anti-social the institution is; how archaic and remote and how worm-eaten. Perhaps we could begin by making crime legal. Nothing is half as attractive if it's legal, and lawyers would be reduced to menial tasks like will-filing and property conveyance and God knows they've got their fingers in *that* lucrative pie to an unnerving degree. They are worse than plumbers for mystifying their work, and anyway we've all got computers now. Conveyancing is a five minute job. It takes the average solicitor five weeks at the very least, so you can see how dishonest they are. I rest my case. I've got them cornered and that makes me nervous.

Blessed are the MEEK

'What is religion, Zeno?'

His head nodded up and down petulantly and then looked sideways giving me a frontal view of a side-mounted eye. It spoke a whole world of reason . . . . . Religion in its widest sense . . . . . it said . . . . . signifies a sensation of reverence which men entertain towards the supernatural being, a supreme presence which controls the powers of nature and is therefore the only power above and beyond man's own ego that he will allow . . . . .

'Pedantic stuff, Zeno!' I suggested.

Zeno turned his back on me, stooped and picked indolently at the brown stubs of grass. The other sheep were jostling and pushing for the food they felt sure was there but could not see. If this two-legged creature hangs around, it must still have something edible on its person – that is their reasoning. All I had was my notebook. Zeno turned again slowly, but hardly confronting me.

. . . . . Do not seek for reason in man's beliefs. They are spontaneous and instinctive. Do not try to rationalise a widespread belief, even though it is reasonable to assume that a belief establishes itself as a necessary deduction of reason . . . . .

'Careful, Zeno, you are trying to play on both sides of the fence but you are still in the orchard,' I said cleverly.

. . . . . And do not think that because you can leave the orchard whenever you like you have found the answers – you've only found the gate . . . . .

I was stunned by this bogus philosophical riposte.

. . . . . Religions have been established on the basis of one man's personal revelation . . . . . Zeno continued . . . . . All religions, in fact. The specific use of the term 'religion' applies to the collective acts and ceremonies which constitute an organised form of devotion. Man needs to be led. He cannot operate wholly as an individual. Man generalises, then unites . . . . .

'That's dangerous talk coming from a sheep,' I sneered. The rest of the flock was no longer interested in my notebook as a source of nourishment and had turned passively in many directions, expecting pastures new and waiting for one of its number to make a positive move.

'You were for the chop, don't forget.' The words rattled from my mouth like nails. 'I nearly didn't buy you,' I blurted impulsively. 'The farmer suggested that you would be more trouble than you were worth and my return would be negligible. But he doesn't realise. Perhaps he is a good farmer and a poor philosopher. That kind of thing can't be measured in wool, yield, lamb chops and foot rot.'

Zeno's eye was now the colour of sheep dip and its square pupil had narrowed to a fine, questioning line.

'But he always talks like that.' I was floundering. 'Apparently because you'll never be a ram – and don't ask me about that, it's beyond me – something about a rubber band around your vitals, causing untold, painful damage. Eventually they just drop off.'

The light went out of Zeno's eye.

. . . . . Did you know this all along? . . . . .

'Only recently, when I asked if I could buy you. It's not important. Farmers are always saying things they don't mean. They live in a world of uncertainty. They complain about the weather and curse the vet. They pay no rates and pray

170

for more subsidies. They are gloomy, disappointed men whose toil has been rendered worthless by a bad crop – a cruel whim of nature. Their wits stand for nothing. Their humour turns as brown as the earth. But we are afraid of them because we need them. We need their crops no matter how small and we have come to rely on their resistance to catastrophe and manure on their boots. We forgive them their self-indulgences and the favours showered upon them by petrified governments. They are above man's laws and bow only to those of nature.'

. . . . . Then why *did* you buy me? . . . . .

Zeno's look was now as hard as frozen turf.

'I thought I was going to get you for nothing. *That's* why! How much do *you* reckon you are worth?'

. . . . . That depends on you. You seem to come and visit me a lot . . . . .

'Well, look – the farmer reckoned I wouldn't get much return on you, what with the problem of disease, foot rot, all that feed you keep eating. That costs money, and since you're no longer a ram you're only good for a bit of wool and 56 lbs of meat. Frankly your yield is limited.'

. . . . . I thought you were my friend . . . . .

'Of course I am, Zeno. I christened you, didn't I? C'mon Zeno, let's work it out.' Zeno cocked his head, quizzically, searching for a hint of compassion. I continued, 'Look, when the farmer came, I *told* you to lie doggo, play sick, get him worried. I was going to say you'd been like it since early that morning. But you didn't, you dumb beast. You charged into that truck like four buffaloes. In fact, I reckon it was *you* who burst that tyre! So don't come whining to me with your

woolly arguments about *our* faults, you stupid, two-faced, four-legged mindless twit. Get back to your work and get that grass down. What d'you think this is, the London School of Economics?'

'Like the sandal tree, shed your perfume on the axe that fells you.' Who said that? Circa 1842.

One may not agree with police methods or other people's beliefs and find police methods difficult to forgive and other people's beliefs difficult to understand, but I think you would find other people's methods far more difficult to stomach and certainly police beliefs more incomprehensible.

Other people's methods would not even be tempered by the clumsy procedure of the law and unless you want to see the return of public lynching of members of your own family on your own front lawn by the light of a flaming cross then support your local police for all their shortcomings.

And police beliefs – well, look here: try to imagine *your* thoughts as you watch a howling mob of self-righteous demonstrators through the toughened plastic of your riot shield and try to believe in the inherent good in *all* mankind.

Never be fooled by the nature of the cause for which people demonstrate. Beneath the thick layer of justification for outbursts against the state there lurks a stranger personal reason within the dark vanity of the soul which cannot be justified, but must be acknowledged.

The police we get are a reflection of the society they are compelled to serve.

The beliefs we indulge in are a reflection of the confusion we are victims of. Who said *that*? Circa 1984.

By God, he's good.

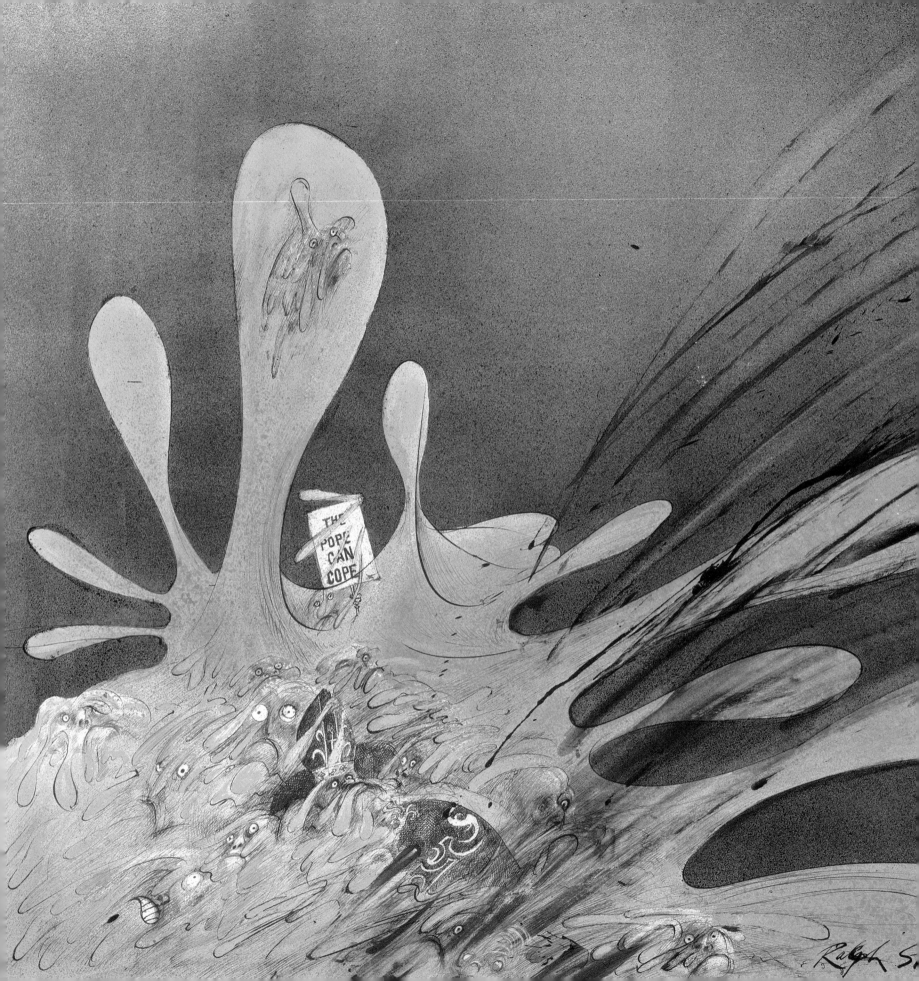

The Gospel according to ST. E. ADman

AND the Lord said, I will destroy man whom I have created from the face of the earth; both man and beast and the creeping thing, and the fowls of the air; for it repenteth me that I have made them. Nay! even the rich and famous in their private jets shall not be saved, for the fountains of the deep will break up and the windows of heaven will open, and behold **GOD**, will send forth in his might a giant custard pie to be upon the earth, and people will stand on one another saying, 'What manner of slapstick GOD is this, who hurleth a mighty custard pie 25,000,000 cubits wide by 10,000,000 cubits high?'

Then men will appear who maketh a fast buck and they will offer Salvation where none is theirs to give, saying, 'Follow us and we will give thee five minutes more of thy time for as little as $1000 down — but none is theirs to give..... So there!

Los Angeles, sprawling monument to a mutant culture. Sunset Strip in the land of concrete breeze blocks, hollow freakishness and radical sleaze.

I remember with affection and awe a sight I have seen many times from a poolside perch at a friend's house high up on the crazy slopes of Beverly Hills. As the evening sun casts orange black shadows through the haze of a hot landscape, a strange flat purple shroud reveals itself – a hovering, silent menace of photochemical smog. Angelenos are almost proud of it. It has been there so long. The smog is to Los Angeles as the pyramids are to Egypt. Ominously beautiful, it unites 4,083 square miles of startling contrast and watches over a population of reeking rich and wretched poor whose greatest industry spins dreams for the whole world and whose excesses spew out of the film sets and on to the streets reassembling themselves like scenery in an animated cartoon.

I am a stranger in this papier mâché world, but I feel its plastic heartbeat and I can see its blood glow in neon tubes. I see also its huge joke and I laugh but to myself, for I know it is somebody's religion and must be recognised as such.

The essence of this culture is the speed with which it can erect its ikons and reinvent itself daily. To be unreal is to acknowledge its cardinal rule: anything is possible.

They have built the Tower of Babel up to heaven – sideways. And they are crossing the desert in a bid to reach hell.

Conventional good taste does not startle and therefore has no place here. Within its own context Los Angeles does not need to concern itself with good or bad taste, but simply flavours of the month. Wildness rules and craves a wilder theme to pump its own adrenalin. Life must be up. There is no time for reflection.

Everything erected has a purpose and must state its case

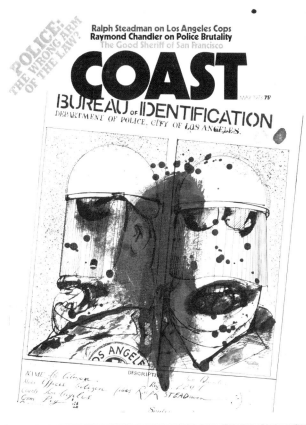

like an exploding bomb if it is to survive. It must be quick or tomorrow it will be something else entirely.

Three kinds of creatures live best in Los Angeles – crazy people, cockroaches and rats, and they all must live somewhere.

Inside the hollow caverns of monstrous brown donuts, winsome cartoon characters and plaster-bound, square-jawed hamburger eaters lurk the refugees from the sterilised world of breakfast coffee shops, brunch joints and cool, dark cocktail bars down below. It's the only place left for them to go and if they can't make it to the desert they must be content to live in these bizarre hidey-holes with front doors that glow with good news neon messages declaring the best Mexican Tacos, all-nite massage, 365-day laundromat and Christ is Risen. Out of sight and out of mind they would not dare to rub shoulders with the creatures on two legs who use tactics not unlike their own but with far more ruthless cunning.

Life down below is lived at a desperate pitch that would leave the average rat steaming like an old horse and a cockroach choking on its back.

There is laughter, of course, but it rises to cackling fever pitch to the sound of cascading money too many times a day, and that means nothing to a rat.

The instant and the new are the mainsprings that have created an art form with no roots in the sand, no rules and an aesthetic yardstick forged only by the power of what it has to sell. But it all had to start somehow and while the endless stream of pioneer sod-busters who left Independence, Missouri, in the early 1840s

and made it finally to the Pacific West didn't actually start this trend in tackiness and Technicolor bawd, they may have sown those early seeds.

They were, after all, eager desperate souls, hungry for land and prosperity, otherwise they would never have attempted such a trek in the first place. They must have been acquisitive and prepared to suffer hellish privations and try anything – which could be construed as a sterling quality, whatever it finally wrought – and they can hardly be blamed directly for the Disneyland that grew up under the name of Los Angeles. They were in search of the fertile earthly paradise, the God-given reward for pitting their courage against the wilderness. Instead, they found a desert with little or no water. This is no problem at all if you know where to look and if you have just travelled 2,000 miles and crossed some of the greatest rivers you know where to look. So they tapped the Colorado River with a big pipe 300 miles long and behold, a fertile earthly paradise was born. With near tropical weather and limitless water on tap the place sprouted like an Amazonian jungle.

With the coming of the huddled masses, the discovery of oil, the invention of the internal combustion engine and cinematography, instant prosperity and the wildest of dreams were realised with a speed which the Angelenos have not made the slightest effort to stem. Today the place screams like a punkish whore bedecked with more layers of fluorescent colour and chrome plated kitsch than a monster Wurlitzer.

Its shapes owe nothing to any ideal but its own. If you are selling hot dogs then that is the perfect shape for a building and it tells the masses outside exactly what you are selling, so you don't waste their time. It is the most logical mainline communication system yet devised. All you need to know from an architect, if that's what you would call him, is whether the damn thing will stay up long enough for you to make a fast buck and get the hell out before the last customer has spread his ketchup.

I forgive it all because it is so brutal and so honest and perhaps most because it is so like itself. I even respect it in a certain way as I respect a cobra or a killer whale.

I don't want to live in it or buy it, write a sonnet on the banks of its flowing freeways. I see no romance in the poolside scenery, no substance in the stupefied lives of suntanned figures in a landscape; I take no comfort from the frantic services offered around the clock, feel no warmth in the glow of a liquor store window in the early hours. Maybe I'm already gone. The victim of a glittering drug strewn along a thousand miles of sidewalk. A lousy B-movie actor who struts and frets his hour upon a tacky film set, and then is heard no more.

But the tale he had to tell if only he'd had the chance is already scrawled in swashbuckling neon letters on children's building blocks anywhere you care to look – by the devil's poet laureate himself in the kingdom of the blind where the one-eyed man wears shades and drives a white Cadillac.

HONZA!

Feverish with anticipation before the long journey and waiting to take off for Melbourne and the centenary test I try a couple of practice run-ups to an imaginary wicket situated around the centre toilets on Qantas flight 002, letting fly a couple of mini sugar packets in a series of wicked leg spin twists before being asked to take my seat at silly mid-on, row 42F, and fasten my safety belt.

The captain has got his pads on and is ready to fly.

A half-heated meal of gastric Russian roulette is served. My heart is heavy in the knowledge that England are playing badly. I have the distinct feeling that the game is moving faster than an ostrich being chased by a jeep and that by the time I arrive it will be all over.

I fidget. We're stationary at Frankfurt. Time – 8.45 pm, three hours after take-off from London. Time enough for Australia to have scored at least 191 more runs. The journey stretches out before me to some future date on another calendar. I browse the menu. It is broken down into six sections of

Lillee Lover with hero effigy
Ralph STEADman 16.3.77

Aussie with his ice cold cans.

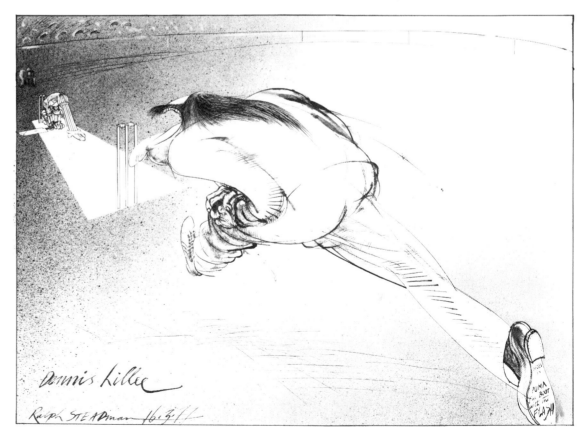

Dennis Lillee
Ralph STEADman 16.3.77

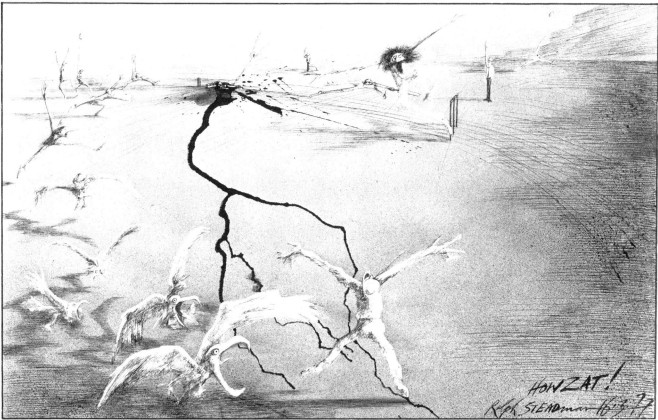

different meals, each one representing a flight sequence and no doubt 60 more runs for Australia or a complete innings for England: Frankfurt/Bahrain, five hours 35 minutes. Dinner is served. Davis out, caught Knott, bowled Greig, sort of thing. Bahrain/Bangkok, a mere six hours five minutes. Breakfast and lunch are served. Walters is batting well and clocks up another 40 runs. Australia's leaping ahead. Bangkok/Singapore, two hours 10 minutes. Game stops for lunch. Then a record seven hours 20 minutes Singapore to Sydney. Ample time for Rodney Marsh to score his century at least and it's a Good Morning Continental Breakfast, chilled fruit cocktail and croissant served with marmalade and strawberry jam. A short last lap to Melbourne and we may be just in time to see the next test series two years hence, arriving there to find the ground empty save for a wizened old groundsman who has forgotten who Dennis Lillee is. We haven't even reached Bahrain yet. Bahrain, Bangkok, Singapore – all merge into one. The flight is interminable. My

life becomes an airborne procession of plastic trays of mould-cast food. I fumble through the newspapers scattered around and read the old scores again. People sit with glazed early morning eyes, or is it afternoon now? The cricket must be over. Australia 493 for 3 retired. England all out for 82, eight men killed, one maimed for life, one with incurable brain damage and the eleventh man refuses to leave the dressing room, locking himself in the toilet with a cricket bat and a half-drunk bottle of Captain Morgan rum. Mass hysteria over an old once-gentlemanly game. Perhaps it was a game and now it's a sport, with all the full-throated blood craving of a Roman arena. People en

masse, whipped to fever pitch over the sight of their men in combat, whom they see as symbols of their national pride. Under its cloak a man can be a beast and be forgiven. He can cry for vengeance and get it.

Cricket was never a spectator sport, but at best a spiritual experience played out by an individual who uses the skill of his body to express himself through reflexes and finely timed strokes. What happens in the pavilions and the stands during this ritual of concentration is of no interest to a committed player. And only he will know the true nature of his satisfaction.

Our age demands that the game should declare itself and join the twentieth century. Externalise! Its participants must play to the gallery or die. Cricket's original aspirations and subtleties must give way to brashness and the instincts of killers to match the vivid attractions of other sports, where the money and vested interests lie and five star national pride is pumped in like a petrol truck filling an underground tank – where the stakes are as high as if one were going to war.

And it's probably all happening in Melbourne at this very moment. The concept is realised, there's money to be made and records to be set up and smashed. A massive dose of tragedy is all that's required now to bring the yahoos out of the dark corners of our minds and send the whole ball game into a new and dangerous dimension.

Singapore. I kill time watching fat proprietors stand about outside their shops at the airport, making sure that the yapping toy dogs and flashing toy police cars stay in line and exactly in front of their particular establishments.

Police cars – ah yes! Melbourne will be alive with them just now, heavily engaged in mopping up activities after the ugly riots following the match. Victorious drunks will be roaming the streets, raping and pillaging the helpless English cricketers and fans invited over for the game.

We take off again for Melbourne, on the last lap of what has been a marathon hiatus. No further news. They have obviously suppressed the true reports of bestial cricket form. I can understand it. It's bad

John Arlott talks CRICKET

181

for the tourist trade. Ah, here comes another face freshener. My face is now as raw as an orang-outang's arse.

We are arriving in Melbourne as the Australians retire at 419 for 9. It's lunchtime on Wednesday and England has the rest of the day and the next to show up the Aussie bowling for what it is – legalised vandalism. Randall is in with Amiss. They have introduced for the first time a dim light of hope for England and play the afternoon through as the shadows creep across the ground like arthritic fingers of doom. Bad light stops play at 5.45 pm with Randall only 13 runs away from his century. If he can keep this up Her Majesty may well get to the match to hear at least once the click of a ball on the willow wand of an English batsman. The gentle sound of Empire. But the seagulls sit around on the manicured green and wait for the end.

The rest is history. The game is lost for exactly the same number of runs we lost by one hundred years ago. What a coincidence! I walk to the gents' toilet deep in thought and relieve myself of everything Australian.

'The gime was reegged, ya knaw thet, don'tyer sport?' confides a roughly hewn Aussie with hair on his inside lip. 'We're steell a bunch of pommie royalists who let Rendell stay een, just to let Queenie drive around in England's finest hour!' I try to hide my face in the wash basin and pretend not to hear. But I *can* hear the crowd in ecstasy beating their seats in the two dollar stands with empty beer cans and Jubilee mugs. It is time to get out. Swarms of them will be pouring on to the pitch lifting the Aussie team shoulder high and trampling the losers underfoot. Still hiding my face in a piece of paper tissue I stumble towards the nearest exit. I can hear the dull sound of cricket bats being broken over English heads and the swish of airborne boomerangs is getting louder. Old colonials cower beneath the seats in the pavilion in a vain attempt to avoid the terror.

John Arlott is whisked away to a secret destination in one of the cars hired for the royal tour of the ground. I feel pretty inconspicuous wearing my souvenir hat with corks on the brim, discreetly humming 'Waltzing Matilda'.

I slowly walk away, sideways, rather like an Aborigine hunting for ostrich eggs. I make the exit a little ahead of the ugly mobs. Settling myself behind a roughly built hut, which has been post office and bric-à-brac shop for the duration of the test, I watch as they emerge. Things are worse than I thought.

Anyone looking vaguely English is trussed up like a scarecrow with a cricket bat and stumps pushed rudely through coat sleeves and across shoulder blades to render him incapable of defending himself. Pads are strapped in threes around both legs at once and the hapless victim is made to hop along beneath an onslaught of cricket balls. Gibes like 'Good on ya, blue!' and 'Let's see ya hop like a wallaby, sport!' fill the evening air, and I find myself watching the most

unbridled display of extra-cricketal activities I've ever witnessed. Australian Stump Goading!

I gasp in horror as an old-timer keels over, clean bowled with an off-spin googlie from a youth who can't be more than fifteen. The skill of his delivery leaves me in no doubt that Australia still has a great cricket future ahead.

I am beginning to feel squeamish at the sight of three stumps simultaneously being eased between a ——

Wallop! All I remember is a starry black-out and when I come to it is nearly dark. The perimeter of the cricket ground looms ominously against the dying day. A pencil-thin shaft of illumination shines vertically into the sky and blurs into a bulbous glow in the clouds gathering over Melbourne. Am I now at last in some celestial state? I do not know that it is only the Queen switching on a beam of light representing the spirit of culture newly inaugurated in Melbourne's arts centre and national gallery.

Three minutes after it is switched on, it is switched off again as Her Majesty leaves to attend a banquet. I think it only fair to point out that this is for economic reasons. The Arts Council of Australia receives only 0.000024 per cent of the national budget and 87 per cent of that is awarded to the Sydney Opera House for its services to tourism and Aboriginal music.

I have seen enough and the lump on my head is throbbing like a ferry boat engine. Bodies lie all around like so much flotsam on a deserted beach. I shrug. That's cricket, I guess. Pulling my cork-lined hat down hard I slink into the lobby of my hotel, collect my baggage and check out in a whisper. I am prepared to sleep on a bench at the airport and catch the next available plane out rather than hang around in this place to become another stump victim. Because to my mind that certainly ain't cricket.

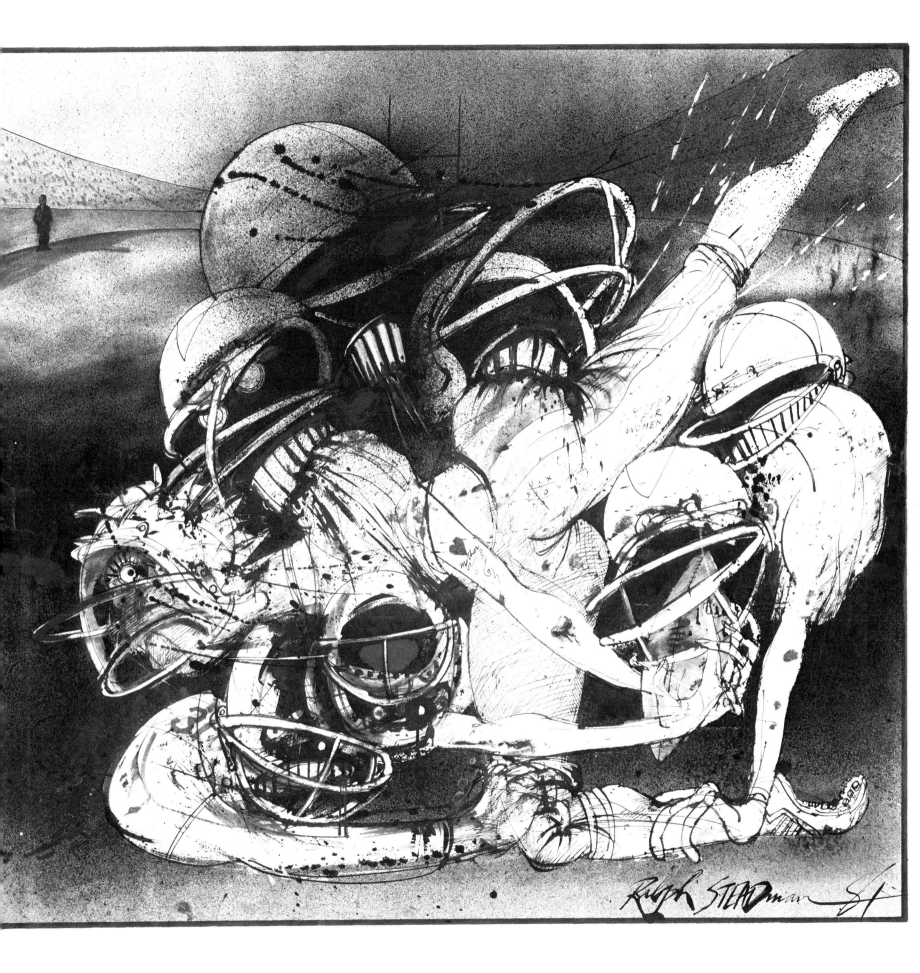

Ralph STEADman

Natural ENEMY

NATURE NOTE

1.00 pm February 15, 1984

I have just watched a magpie and a seagull fighting in mid air, screeching and screaming at each other. They have nothing in common except that they can both fly.

A seagull is a scavenger. A magpie is a hoarder and hates the sea. Why were they fighting? Whose territory was threatened? What is so terrifying about another's presence.

It is a perfect example of misunderstanding and let it be a lesson to us all, for neither party gained a single extra morsel of air space or explained his position.

But they both benefited. They both exercised their lungs and that is the quintessential purpose of a damn good demonstration on the streets.

CAN YOU BEAR TO LOOK THIS WHALE IN THE EYE?

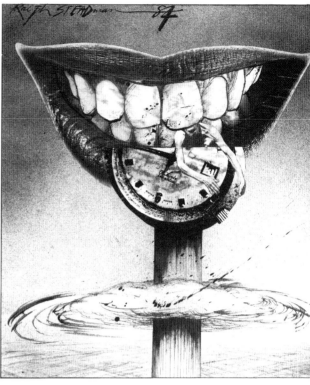

BANG! µ @ µ : # # ★ ½ # ★ ? ? ★ ½ # ½) % & $ £ ½ ★ ★ ★ ★ ? + . That + 's what. I have a secret and YOU wont know anything about it and by the time I get to the end of this high speed sentence it may be all over and you wont even get to read iteven if I cut out allthe ticks and punctuation it will get you before you can say pass it over here e its that fast and if your in the middle of itdont even bother to sneeze ifyou feel one coming on the only people who will get away with it are airline passengers and russian cosmonauts ontheir way to mars but they'll be up the proverbial without a paddle unless their are some lovely women on that planet to start civilisation all over again providing they were that friendlyand anyway there isnt that much room even on a wide bodied jet to allow for that kind of carry on at 20000 feetand what for anyway because they'll have to come down sometimeDont even think about it but you cant help it sometimes just like you cant help thinking about space and what's beyond it and then what's beyond thatand so on nothing it drives people mad and why god made flies and then you think that perhaps hes made a mistake after alland hes realising OK peace to the lot of you and if you havent already let it off well dont noteven as a joke .... BAA____!

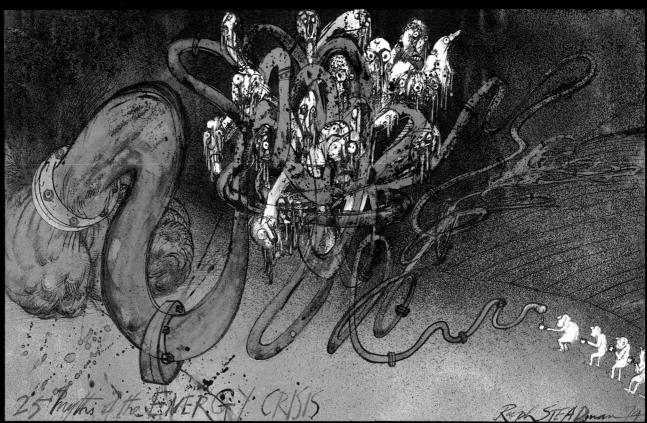

25 Myths of the ENERGY CRISIS   Ralph STEADman 74

Formula 1.

Belgium set me thinking. So many cheap cars and cobblestones. The smell of burnt rubber and high octane fuel. I only wanted to know how it looked as a drawing, so I sat down on a grass verge behind a glittering Formula I black and yellow chariot. Underneath, finely honed metal, turned to perfection. Rods of varying sizes sprang from the dark belly of the body and clamped themselves on to hub lugs, machine-faced sprockets and thrung bolts. Shafts of shimmering silver bored holes into gleaming discs like sun piercing cathedral windows, re-emerging to thrust apart a ——

'Hey, you! What you doin' here?'

'Oh, I'm just trying to draw this wonderful machinery.'

'Er, who d'you work for?'

'Well, I'm an artist, here on assignment to, er –'

'You some kind of industrial designer? I mean, it's not usual. That's our secret back axle you're drawing there. Who d'you say you work for?'

'I didn't. It's a *Radio Times* assignment.'

'Radio. They don't show drawings on the radio. Are you sure you're not some kind of spy?'

'*Radio Times*. It's a magazine. I'm drawing for an article. This sketch will help me with the finished drawing.'

'I'd prefer it if you didn't

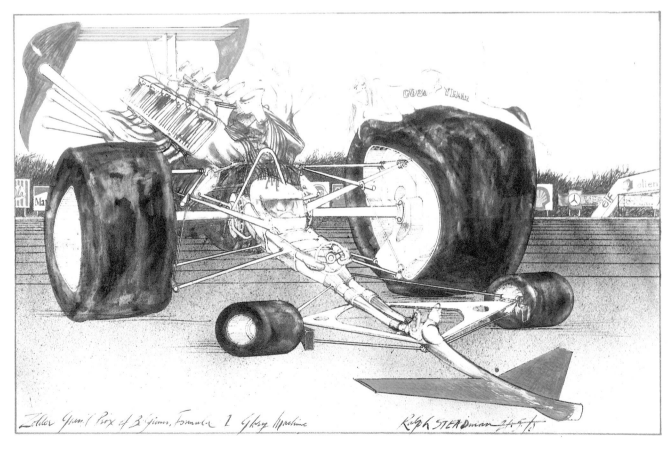

draw. You've got a camera there. I don't mind cameras. But drawing – well!' He drew breath in through his teeth. 'You can't be too careful these days.'

'Sorry!'

Hmm. Doesn't say much for modern photography.

Hawaii

Hawaii is, and has always been, a Garden of Eden, lush with raven black rock over land which once thrived as green and rampant as an English meadow. It used to be nothing at all, not even land. It is the last great island to date to be born along the ridge known as the Polynesian Archipelago. Born in thrusting turmoil – and aren't we all, thrusting and turmoiling until the day we die.

I accepted the black rock as a friend because I looked upon it as the afterbirth of a long labour. Something protective and not yet ready to produce its child – the real island of Hawaii. From time to time tiny green spondules thrust up between the craggy sharp liquorice surfaces referred to as real estate by those on the island called the dark ones. Those who barter, sell and cheat. About once every four years the beautiful but treacherous Goddess Pele of the volcanoes, crossed in love, screams out and one hundred acres of black gold spews from orange-red eyes of fire, bubbling and oozing downhill on the south side of Hawaii. That's about another 20 million dollars in the deep pockets of those who go there for gain. The dark ones. The Goddess rides the liquid fortune blessing it with her black incantations. She is indeed the patron saint of Realty. But the lives of those are also changed who wake up that morning and find this effluent filling their kitchens as well as at least another acre of their back yards. God be with them, for they stay put and hold their ground as true pioneers, planting and nurturing and making fertile. Not so, the dark ones. They plan and scheme, buying, selling and prospering beyond reason. If they plant anything at all it is only a boundary marker between one lot and the next – which gave me the very idea I needed to clean up.

Boundary markers! I called them Terrus Pele Vindictavus, otherwise known as the Green Flash. Hardy annuals grown out of rock and as hungry and mean as an army of soldier ants. Not only do they grow impenetrable boundaries but they cover valuable ground too, relentlessly, with their own kind of greed, hungry for anything they can find amongst the crevices and corners of the black rock.

I was eager to see if my plan would work. I found the prototype perched on a bald jutting plateau with its roots spreadeagled over the edges, a green octopus quivering as the roots searched for food where none was visible to the naked eye. The moment I saw it, the sun was setting over the Western Pacific and flashed green for an instant. This is the spectrum phenomenon caused by the effect of low intense light through the hazy evening hemisphere. Green flash! Hundreds were dotted around in the same manner – always on some barren bald pate, yet these little buggers thrived like Saracen hordes.

I gazed upon them with the poker dead eye of one who knows he has a royal flush.

The dark ones were so desperate to protect their new-gotten areas of blackness that they fell for my marketing pitch as if I were offering free drugs.

I simply put up a sign on an undeveloped piece of sacred Hawaiian burial ground which said: 'Obtrusive and impenetrable barriers for sale at property protecting prices. Apply: Box 2313, Kailua Kona, Hawaii 94726.'

The response at first was wary but curiosity and fear gradually overcame caution. People can't resist a deal which reinforces the territorial prerogative, the prerogative which a dog uses to preserve a patch where it likes to shit and hide bones.

A dog is traditionally a loyal animal to man. It looks up at him with big, round comforting eyes and never criticises. When you kick it, it finds an excuse to lick your hand. Neighbours are like that if you keep them in their place, which of course is next door. And that's where Terrus Pele Vindictavus, my appalling new plant, is so effective. More, you can train it to act like a dog. You can make it beg or attack at will.

The more strident plants had begun to write things, ominously shaping themselves into phrases like 'Get lost' and 'OK buster, that's

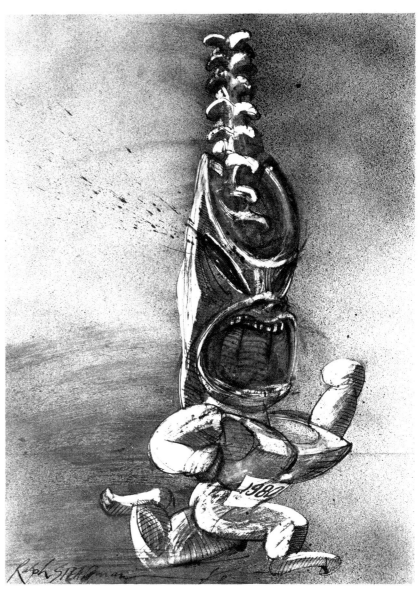

far enough.' The fiercest one I came across had twisted itself into a cry from the blackest heart: 'I was here first.'

North Pacific marine forecast. Moderate to strong north-east trade winds. North to north-west swells ten feet with fourteen- to twenty-foot breakers on some north-facing beaches. Dull start brightening later and settling. Warm trends developing. Water temp. 72°F., air 82°F.

That kind of forecast around mid-December draws the world's best surfers to the north shores of Oahu, one of the Hawaiian islands. They come for two of the world's great surfing classics. The Duke Kahanamoku at Waimea Beach is named after the royal Hawaiian who revived surfing in the early part of this century. The Hawaiians invented surfing, but in the nineteenth century missionaries arrived and tried to stifle the islanders' love of it because it looked like too much fun.

The second contest, the Banzai Pipeline Masters Surfing Classic, is the one which gets the most attention and takes place along Sunset Beach about another two miles down the same coastline. Many a surfer has seen his last sunset right there. The authorities broadcast constant warnings to the public not to chuck themselves into these boiling waters unless they know exactly what they're going to do next. The force of the suction that a wave creates as it pulls back from the shore is enough by itself to drag you under for the last time. So I paddled.

Surfing is not a sport. It's a religion whose worshippers are golden brown, suntan oil slicked Rasputins and body-shaved Dulux dogs versus white raging foam with the energy of 3,000 miles of high swell on the world's biggest ocean. Brave but dumb. In the last couple of years, Punk has created its own styles in high chic. Black leather wetsuits with studs, cheap masks, tattooed white bodies and rough handsewn patchwork trousers. Surf Punk Pop makes songs like 'Bird Bathroom' and 'Beercan Beach'.

There is nothing before you but pure poetry, amazing luck or savage black

rocks. Certain death if you don't cut back in the nick of time.

A championship proceeds only when the weather conditions are right, producing monstrous thunderers wrought by the high swell. Ideally there will be TV cameras, helicopters and an efficient Coke and hot dog stand to feed the people.

Nothing is guaranteed, not even life itself which is part of the attraction. Perhaps the fresh air too, but mostly the smell of blood. How big is how brave and how skilful.

A lull shows up figures. Bobbing flotsam on brightly coloured boards, like survivors from a shipwreck, and in this sea all men are equal.

Suddenly, white tips form and crumble down over a developing smooth curved chasm of blue.

A rider is announced on a Tannoy only as he appears over the lip – the one who didn't just get on a wave but grabbed it like a shark grabs meat and he's off down to the devil and if he's skilful enough and lucky, he may find himself riding inside an awesome barrel with high G forces holding him against the most complex and volatile surface one can ever imagine.

'There is no time to think,' a surfer told me, 'it's all reflex action – that's why you must devote your life to it and practise. Reading waves and currents is like reading busy music. It's not a casual affair.'

What we the spectators see can never compare with what the surfer feels far from the shore and suddenly on the wave, sliding down curved frosted glass – a big roller indifferent to you and only doing what it has to do, obeying the law of gravity and thundering down on itself.

It is not a religion. It's Russian Roulette.

The LAST Walt

ALIGHT HERE FOR THE LAND OF SCREAMING KIDS AND TIRED FEET

People walk around here on dollar crutches. Difficult to be independent. Has a nice soporific effect but I long for the self-caught fish, the fire amongst stones, a free, running river and a bottle of vin ordinaire. Nature's own shot of bourbon.

We sit petrified, having bought tickets to go on eleven things. We've got to go on them otherwise we haven't done Disneyland – and anyway it's a waste of money if you don't use them. But I am looking forward to Mrs Toad's Wild Ride.

Let's start – first stop Sleeping Beauty's Castle.

It's over, and I'm so thrilled about one thing – most people love to do what I hate, like shoving and pushing to get a Wild West burger. Queueing for an hour to get on a Matterhorn bobsled and preferring Autopia to walking through the way out turnstile.

But imagine the horror when we realise you can't get a beer in the whole damn phantasmagoria – just Coke, coffee or lemon tea.

That shortened our chances of staying the course to something like 11 to 7.

But in a fine British way, we stuck at it and somewhere in all that hot sweaty composition building complex and phoney jungle something felt good. It may just have been familiar old Mickey. I would have liked it even less if he hadn't been there.

Gradually, the circus of people clamouring for canned amusement took on the real spirit of Disneyland '76. We held back, horrified. It seemed the next best thing to having a polythene bag pulled down hard over our sweating heads.

Writing or drawing things is a desperate situation. Nerves are fraught, taut, caught – where's my notebook? Fuck, I've lost it, oh where is it, oh my God no – I'll look again – it must be here. Here! In this bag – where did you have it last? – in my hand I think. No – not that stupid bar – Ye Olde Pub . . . all those people, hearing my English voice – no barman – thirsty – five minutes before the bus. Where's the goddamn barman? Pour my own, that's OK. No one will care – someone's empty glass on counter – pull tap – take – nothing happens. Ah here you are, OK instead of a Watneys – I'll take a Michelob! Thank you.

'Thank you, sir, have a nice day.' (6.00 pm in the evening!!)

I wonder how many people visit Disneyland in one year? One million? Two? Three? No – no – no –

14 – 000 – 000 people slide through the turnstiles which have to be replaced once every month.

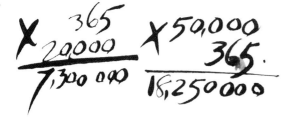

Some pilots are more talkative than others. Some like to give *you* a tourist trip and some just like to say hello.

Thank God that's over – can we get out now, ducky?

If I ever go across the sea to IRELAND

I have never been to Ireland, but it has been my privilege to illustrate *The Poor Mouth* by Ireland's finest comic writer, Flann O'Brien. My backgrounds and my feeling for the types I imagined would inhabit his books were influenced by my visits to Languedoc in south-west France. The people there seem to me to be similar in temperament if not perhaps in humour to the stoical people he portrays, and they don't drink Guinness. The landscapes, however, seem exactly the same because Irish people have told me so and one thing the Irish don't do well is lie about their own country. Lawrence Durrell, who *has* been to Ireland, told me, 'You get the sensation that you are going to meet a Yeats on every street corner' – but sadly, he didn't. Never mind. Lovely people. Not too many Dickenses over here either, come to think of it.

Gardening Hint No. 20

You wouldn't expect Penelope Proust suddenly to come out with 'My idea of a garden is something to sit in,' would you? You're more likely to expect that sort of bone idle comment from some gin-soaked patsy in a deck chair waiting for a blood transfusion. But there it was.

Penelope Proust, by the way, in case you didn't know, is captain of the Olympic Gardening Team representing Britain in 1976, author of The Delicate Art of Pruning, Simple Soil Science *and* Tractors: A History of Soviet Agriculture. *So naturally there must be more to a statement like that than meets the eye – you don't get where she's got without knowing a thing or two. I mean, I'm only the digger on the team and I'm pretty hot.*

I didn't pursue it just then but decided to do a bit of scouting on the quiet and watch her work.

I pulled up an Elaeagnus Pungens noted for its screening value and set up a lookout at the northwest corner of her two-acre garden in fashionable Cockfosters, the great northern outpost of London's Piccadilly Line. She was just emerging from her Marcel Jasen-style tropical conservatory pushing a wheelbarrow containing four huge sacks of humus fertiliser, pruning shears, a trowel, a Zippo lighter and four sticks of dynamite.

With the deliberate motion of a well-practised gardener, she moves gracefully from corner to corner and proceeds as follows: With the trowel

James Joyce repairing Semmets for Jesuit priests.

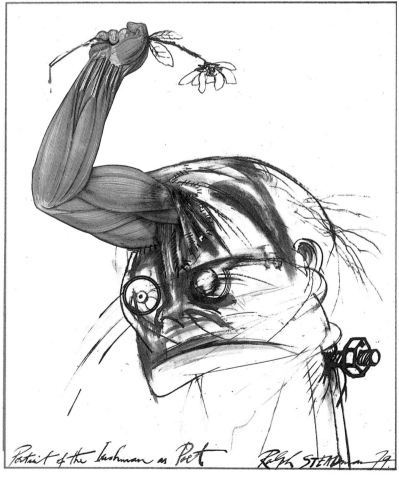

Portrait of the Irishman as Poet

Ralph STEADman 79

she digs a hole in the topsoil 12 inches deep and nine inches wide; at the bottom of each hole she places six inches of humus, followed by one stick of dynamite. Gently she replaces the soil around the stick and firms it with the tips of her fingers and lays one bag of humus over all. She then takes the pruning shears and smartly snips the cordite fuse to a specific length (three feet six inches, for those who try this method, reducing to 11½ inches on the fourth stick), giving simultaneous coition and time to get the hell out of a two-acre plot. (For smaller gardens you would have to experiment and in small backyards you would probably need only one stick anyway. No problem there!) When the dust settles she's around that garden with the pruning shears again, tidying up blown-off branches, etc. Then a nice Irish labourer she has found who has his own rake smooths the debris and pulverised vegetation about. Zippo. Before you can say 'Seed Catalogue 1975' she's reclining in the conservatory, planning a splendid show of annuals for next year.

A word of warning – don't shelter behind an Elaeagnus Pungens for protection or you are likely to get raked over too. Next time, slugs.

Give peas a chance.

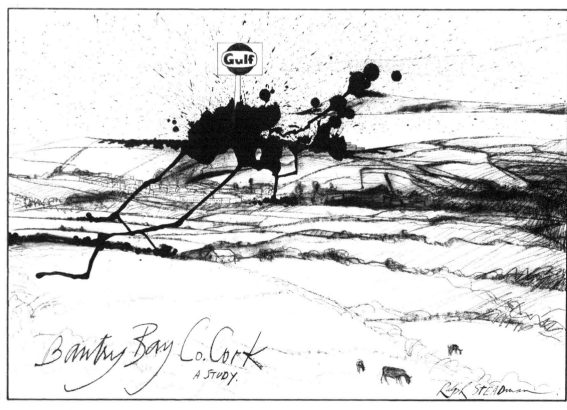

Bantry Bay Co. Cork
A STUDY.

Ralph STEADman

198

NO COUGHING MATTER

All of us have more than a passing fear of medical matters. My difficulty has been to find a reasonable GP. Your average doctor is really not the sort of person to start blathering to about the kind of things I suffer from.

Weird looks are what I have been getting and a hurried glance at the watch to indicate tactfully that there are other patients waiting. There's nothing wrong, they keep telling me. You imagine things. You're a lucky man. You should find something to occupy your mind. Take up squash or medieval jousting. Give up smoking and drinking. Go to bed early. I try describing my intangible fears, but it takes too long and they start getting up, stretching and scratching. Some of them begin telling *their* problems but that's the last thing you want to hear. Some doctors have got horrible problems and that's why they are doctors. They feel that if they live in the eye of a hurricane it will pass them by and leave them purified.

They are simple people just like us and the more of them you meet, the more you realise we're all in trouble. They do some clever things with vital innards and I admire them for it, but they can't deal with the intangible. The nameless fears of our twisted lives. The dank horrors of an unforgotten experience. The creeping phobias that are so real when you are suffering them, but hollow self-indulgence when you are trying to describe them to your favourite GP.

This good soul will side-step the issue by relating cases just like yours, who came into the surgery in a fearful state sweating and palpitating like hung pigs, until he, your favourite GP, told them to pull themselves together and go to night school, or apply to join an over-35 Overland vacation trek out of Morocco. He'll even offer pamphlets for you to take away and browse over, and that's the kind of thing that gets you completely confused. All you want is a chance to pour out your heart, and there you are getting all excited and hot-footing it to Thomas Cook's, buying billycans and khaki shorts.

You don't get a chance to explain those awful tremors you've been getting between bouts of floating sensations and numbness and how people in front of you seem to shimmer and walk through you as though they are part of your dream. Worst of all, he asks you how your family is and whether you've all had mumps whilst ever so gently easing you towards the door. Then you're outside among all those other poor devils with real illnesses sprouting all over the place and

you know he's going to listen to them for hours because their complaints are tangible, even visible.

But out in the street you feel better. You feel great. It's been a real tonic! There's a bounce in your walk and the pub's just across the road. Time for a quick one, though the doctor said you shouldn't drink with the pills. You haven't got them yet, so there's no harm in a small one. You can drink it whilst waiting for your prescription.

STEADman

"I do hope we're not going to hurt each other, Mr. Throbdent"

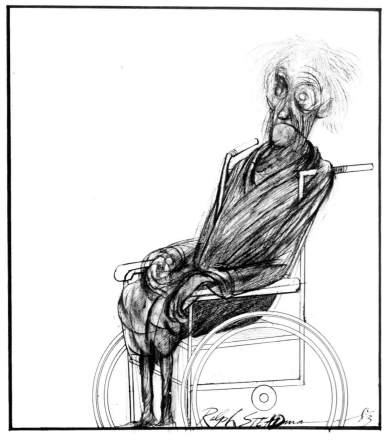

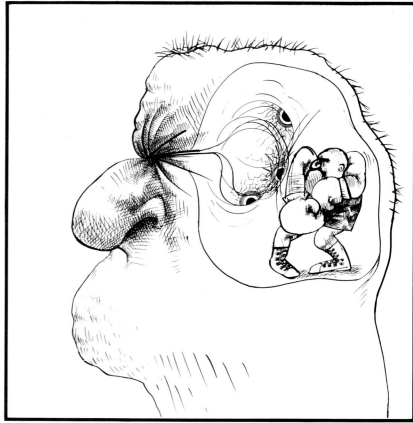

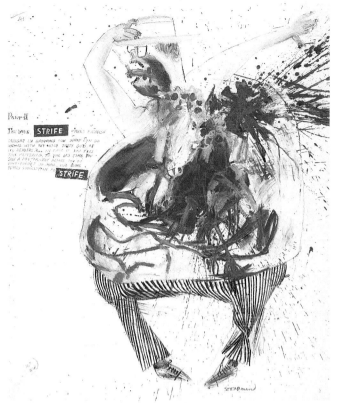

During my wife's hospitalisation, certain complications arose which in the early stages were left unmentioned by the doctors for their own reasons. Things that ultimately, I decided, I could do nothing about but I could get cross.

On a recent visit to the hospital and following many phone calls, during which time my medical knowledge developed quite considerably, I began quizzing a young lady doctor and laying the law on the line. At this point I was not prepared to gamble my wife's life on the strength of a system we would wish to uphold for idealistic reasons. If necessary I would go private. There comes a point when it's every man for himself and you do whatever you can possibly do to obtain the best results. Principles and beliefs go straight through the window when a loved one is in danger. My blood was up and my head was clear. The doctor was visibly taken aback and was continually averting her gaze downwards. I was obviously a man to be reckoned with. Another doctor emerged from a staff office on the same corridor and approached me.

'Mr Steadman?' He offered his hand politely. I took it and a moment later found myself propelled towards him with a swift jerk – eyeball to eyeball.

'Your flies arc undone, old chap,' he whispered fervently. He was right.

It was two hours later when the irony of his remark was revealed by what my wife had to say from her hospital bed.

'Honestly, those doctors,' she said. 'He was half way through his inspection of my lower region, waggling his finger about up my backside and discussing the weather with the nurse and where he was going to eat that evening, all at the same time. He was so casual.'

It left me wondering. At which point does concern for decorum begin and end – with my flies or up my wife's bottom?

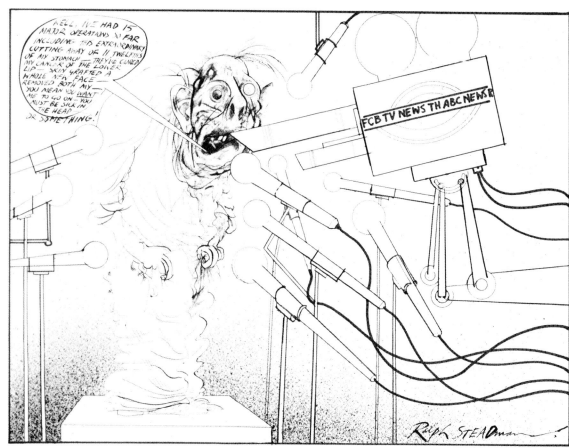

Eating Out

OUTRAGED HOST (TO GUEST WHO HAS INADVERTENTLY PERPETRATED AN EMBARRASSING HISTRIONIC EFFECT): "Dammit man, you've just farted in front of my wife".

DEFAULTING GUEST (NONCHALANTLY): "I do apologise, my dear fellow. I didn't realise it was her turn".

There is a lot to be said for Artists' Power. That they too have been traditionally restrained, like women, from indulging in anything other than what it is they are supposed to do. In the case of women, they have been child-bearing, cleaning, home-making, love-giving buffers, upon which men could replenish themselves before launching out once more to seek their destiny.

In the case of artists, the burden is role-bearing. Strict adherence is required to coded behaviour patterns evolved over centuries by society's official artist watchers. They, the artist watchers, have come to the conclusion that artists do certain things and therefore that's all they should do. They take orders. They feed the souls of those who run the show – within boundaries. This enables the artist to feel as free as he wants to be, and indulge his wilder fantasies. As long as he is seen to be safe in his pigeon-hole, engrossed in his personal activity, society will smile indulgently. He may even be rewarded.

Writers do not suffer such indignities. They have always been regarded as the purveyors of usable knowledge. The hidden persuaders, the architects of ideologies and legal documents who are qualified to write their own contracts. They have a way with words. An artist's work is ephemeral and unearthly; remote and personal, to be enjoyed only in an arena of society's choice. There they are safely contained. Artists are, like actors and jesters, given to role-playing. They follow the script or improvise, by design. Not so the writers. They have discovered who they are, and not merely who they are supposed to be. Artists are fools. There is more to their lives than a pat on the head. If there are people out there shaping our futures, then artists are people too.

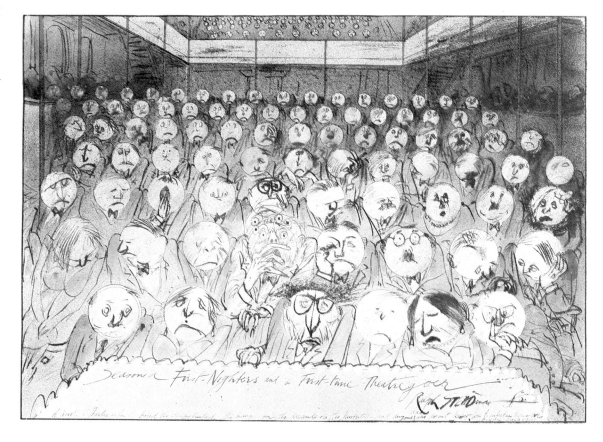

Seasoned First-Nighters and a First-time Theatregoer

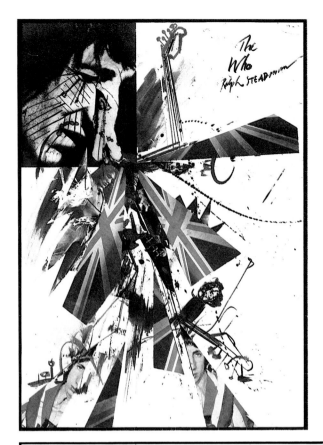

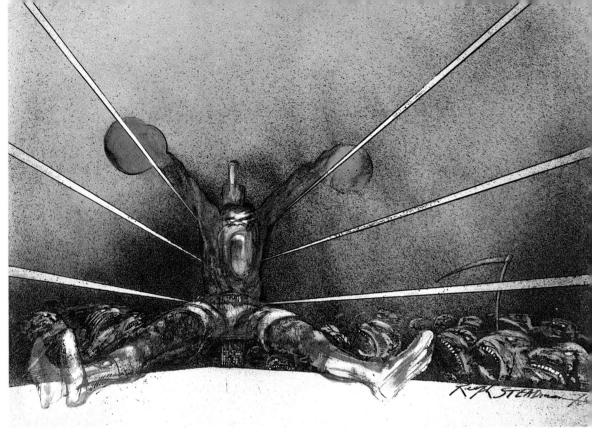

Gardening Hint No. 31

It hadn't mattered until yesterday that whenever I thought about money it had nothing to do with gardening. But yesterday I got this gigantic ground rent demand for my allotment – my beloved piece of God's little acre along the lower slopes of West Brompton Crematorium – pay up or get out. An area that had merely been a dumping ground for fifty gas cookers, 300 tubular steel office chairs, a Buick hub-cap, an ice-box, fourteen galvanised water tanks and a Volkswagen shell was now a viable proposition for somebody on the council.

The increase was due, as Councillor Hennessy Browne with an e put it, 'to heavier overheads, a new swimming pool and a superb new car park over the old graveyard to cater for a magnificent Bingo Hall and a prize-winning football ground.

'There isn't much call for a graveyard these days,' said Councillor Hennessy Browne with an e, 'people aren't dying so much. The air is cleaner. Our borough is on the up and Fulham is about to win the Cup Final. People can breathe again and walk tall.' He had in fact planned to turn the whole gruesome area into an activity playground. Councillor Hennessy Browne with an e didn't quite know why things looked brighter and smelt fresher but had an idea it was something to do with the new highway he had proposed and had bulldozed through Hampstead Garden Suburb to avoid congestion at Fulham Broadway.

Might I just interpolate at this moment and say that I have modest reason to believe that why our air is cleaner is because of my allotment. It is a monolithic growth. My army of green foliage and healthy leaf development is beyond reproach, thanks to my neighbours the stiffs who lie three foot to my right and six foot under and provide me with the finest fertiliser in the history of the world.

If I wanted to survive, and I did, I

needed money to buy the bastards out, not grass seed but big money. There was only one thing for it – write a song about it – get it down, get it played with my own direction, own production and orchestration to save money and ensure success (thank God I took music and art instead of Latin at school) and with a little help from my friends on the council I'd be home and dry, and the concrete loving enemy would be driven back by the war song of the garden republic. Without keeping you on tenterhooks any longer, here is my song:

> Deep soil gotta hit hard rock
> If I'm gonna satisfy my needs
> Deep soil gotta dig till I hit it
> If I'm gonna make a hit with my seeds
> Making out and digging endlessleeeeeeeeee
>
> (Riff with) Hard rock you gotta find it down in deep soil strike oil-l-l-l deep soil-l-l-l-l-l-l-l-l-l-l-l-l-l-l-l-l-l-l-l-l-l-l-l-l-l-l-l-l-l-l
> Rock on hard. Yeh! Hit it! Hard rock hard rock hard rock hard rock hard rock hard rock hard rock hard rock hard rock etc and repeat
> © Steam Songs 1975

If you can pick up my metre, well great, but try it on your plants first with the acoustic guitar – I think they're going to like it but I'm not so sure about people. They do have funny ways.

Your lilies should be shooting up well but watch for botrytis. Have a nice summer.

Next time: Plants that thrive in a recording studio.

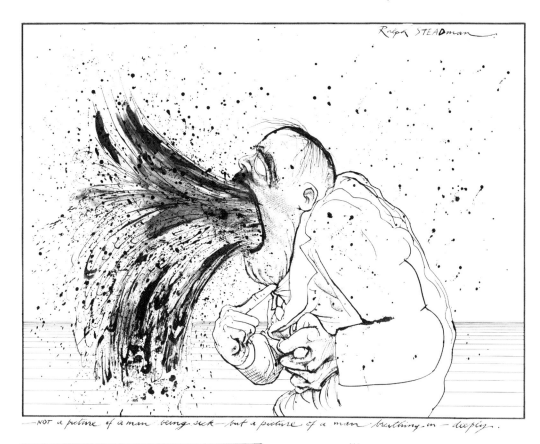

— not a picture of a man being sick – but a picture of a man breathing in – deeply.

A pedestrian said to the Schnorrer, 'Give you a nickel??? Why?? Why don't you go to work? You've got the arms and legs of a horse.'

'Ha!' cried the Schnorrer. 'For one lousy nickel, am I supposed to cut off my arms and legs??'

Your health comes first – you can always hang yourself later.

One father can support ten children – but ten children don't seem to be enough to support one father.

For the first time Mrs Samuelson went to a gynaecologist. 'Now please take off your clothes,' said the doctor.
'My clothes??'
'Yes.'
'Listen – does your mother know how you make a living?'

Two Martians land in America and happen to meet.
'What's your name?' asks the first.
'4286. What's yours?'
'3359.'
'That's funny, you don't look Jewish.'

When a Jewish farmer eats a chicken one of them is sick.

Hitler shrieked, 'Who is responsible for all our troubles?'
'The bicycle riders,' shouted Mr Cohen.
'Why the bicycle riders?' demanded Hitler.
'Why the Jews?' replied Mr Cohen.

'I never drink. In front of children I don't believe and when they're away – who needs it?'

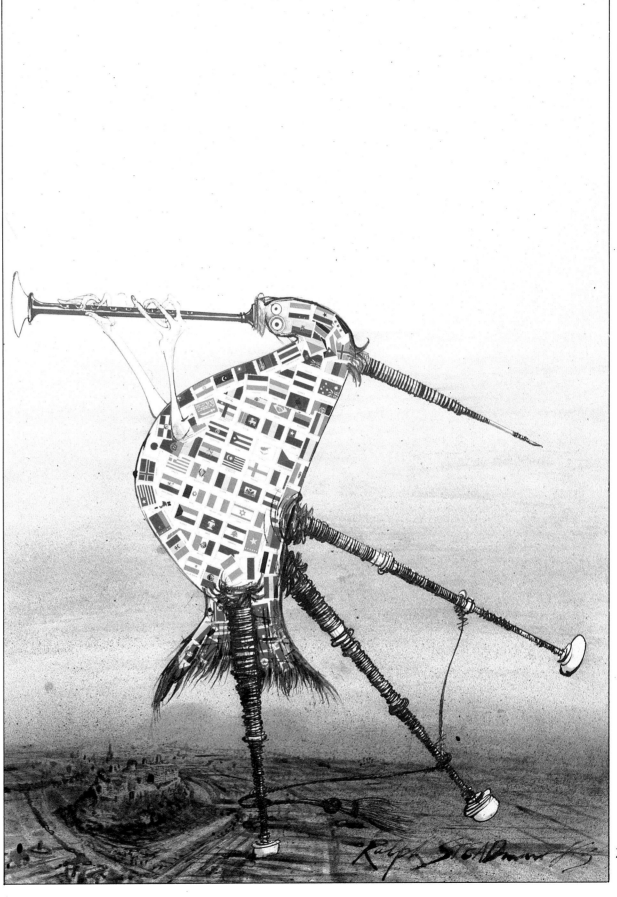

209

The Promised Land

Sunday November 20, 1977. I am invited by the Friends of Israel to visit their country. I am to be met by Mrs Simulian.

'Sadat has arrived in Jerusalem and, ladies and gentlemen, we have arrived in Tel Aviv.' Everybody claps. Mrs Simulian is not there.

The roads around Jerusalem are blocked. I pay off the cabby and walk to the Mishkenot where I am staying.

There is an air of hushed reverence over the place. Everyone is watching Sadat on TV. He's visiting the Holocaust museums.

My first walk around takes in the Wailing Wall, the Jaffa Gate, a view towards the Dead Sea, the King David Hotel and countless police cordons. Being unable to get inside the parliament I watch on TV. Coffee is served and amongst the odd shsh! and shuffle the events unfold.

Jerusalem during Sadat's visit has about it a mixture of reverence and nervousness. They are obviously proud of the event and thrilled and apprehensive. They hope as fervently as children waiting for Christmas that though they cannot expect the moon, perhaps a tiny miracle may result from the special meeting of the Knesset.

Monday November 21. We do not start out from Jerusalem until 10 am and I should be back for the Sadat press conference by 12 noon.

We leave Jerusalem through the Arab eastern section, taking the road to Jericho. Donkeys carry Arabs side-saddle. The Arabs are clutching cans of oil. What we have, we hold?

New estates are growing up beyond the city limits. Square, easy on the eye buildings made of the local stone. In spite of their solid angularity, they seem to fit into the area. Some are half finished and may remain so. Nobody rushes.

The buildings thin out quite suddenly. Desert area. No green. The landscape is dotted with black goats and bedouin women walking along the side of the road.

On the rises surrounding the road, there are occasional bedouin dwellings – a combination of tent material made from goat hair and rocks, built in the form of a shallow cave. The landscape undulates in sudden bumps and rises. Each slope has been naturally terraced by the movement of goats through the centuries, giving a delicate textured quality to the stark panorama.

Beside the Dead Sea, a lido has been half-heartedly built – it reminds me of disused concrete barracks left by the army in the last war. A small path made of corrugated iron, old boards and raised planks on old chains, leads us in a meander to the water's edge.

Thick layers of salt cover the ground and I dip my hands in the water. It feels oily and strange. It is supposed to have great healing powers for skin complaints. My hands take ages to dry. In fact it's rather like covering yourself in too much hand cream which won't rub into the skin. The taste is very bitter. A cut on my hand stings.

We get back rather late for the press conference. Watching it on

210

closed circuit TV I realise it is really not what I came here to see.

At 3 pm Pearl Silver, my guide, calls for me to start the tour of Jerusalem. We see many Ben Gurion characters. Carpets are arranged on the walls of the bridge leading through the Damascus gate as though for sale, but no one around to sell them. The colours zigzag against the old stone. The road is uneven and cobbled. Open at first, it develops into a beehive of arched alleyways lined with small shops selling much the same sort of things that have now appeared in every boutique in Europe. I imagine hordes of potential boutique owners saying, 'Hey, these are great. Imagine, we could clean up if we took a stack of these old bedouin dresses back to London.'

Now, of course, even after bargaining, one pays a high price for ethnic fashion and even then it is not entirely ethnic, but a well studied, market science that the locals have picked up and exploited.

In the Mishkenot restaurant you could be anywhere and not, as we are, on the side of a hill outside the city walls in an area made historic and sacred by the efforts of one man, Moses Montefiore, who carved a home for Jews out of a piece of waste land over a hundred years ago.

I suppose as the Turks and Armenians built new walls and floors over the Greek remains of the early settlements in Jerusalem, so this will also change and one day make way for a thought bank or a beaming station in the twenty-second century.

Tuesday November 22. Today for the first time I see a real cross-section of Jerusalem. From the Mount of Olives we look down on the whole panorama. The Golden Dome mosque sticks out like a birthday cake on a rubbish dump. The impression is temporary. Gradually the prismatic effect of complicated building clusters imposes its own wonderful sensation on the eye. If you cast your eyes sideways and look at a camel sitting nonchalantly on the pavement and then back to the city and back to the camel again, you will see that he is probably watching and that he thinks he has as much right to be on the pavement at a bus stop

Ethiopian Priests on the Roof of the Holy Sepulchre, Jerusalem Ralph STEADman

211

as an Israeli Kibbutz has to be on the West Bank.

From there to Mount Scopus for the most breathtaking change so far. A panoramic view that cuts off my idea of cosiness. Rippling curves zoom away from the eye into a heat haze in the land of nowhere.

I move into it down a steep slope and find a bedouin tent nestled beside what looks like an old army lookout. The bedouin is returning with some water for his goats. He marshals them together to drink.

Then, as though conscious of my presence, he stands in various poses by his tent. His goats are on top of the lookout and I gradually get closer and more confident. He asks for a cigarette and proudly stands smoking it whilst I draw him. Inside his tent he keeps nothing but old boxes, a few blankets and several chickens. The tent itself is crudely sewn up with old sacks, thick bits of canvas and polythene sheets. Rather a sad sight. There are no other occupants. He accepts my interest as though he was expecting me to arrive this very morning.

We then drive to the most oppressive region I have ever seen. The Mea-sherim, the Hasidic Jewish quarter where orthodox Jews exaggerate a stagnant way of life to nauseating proportions. From birth to death the wisdom of the Talmud is their guide and their clothes a uniform of crushing dreariness.

Their wives remind me of East Enders with their hair in curlers under a headscarf 'keeping it in' for the Saturday dance. In the Yeshivah school, for all the world like Wandsworth prison, the children study Talmudic wisdom, provided by the old and infirm. Age has broken down their formal attitude and bowed the head. Orthodoxy has a human shape again.

Back through the Damascus gate we roam the arched streets and climb out of the bustle on to the roof of the Holy Sepulchre. Home for the Ethiopian monks who languish in a subtle grey courtyard like petrified figures in a landscape. Their black elegance is enhanced by their tallness and good features. A vision of peace. The shrine is surrounded on all sides by the Christian religion of the Eastern world. The Armenians are underneath. It is alleged to be the site of Calvary, hence the exploitation of the surrounding real estate.

At the Golden Dome on Temple Mount we remove our shoes and enter. This is the Arabs' own holy place, rich in mosaic and patterned tiling and with a monstrous piece of sacred stone in the middle surrounded by a protective fence of solid oak. Methuselah is believed to have leapt to heaven from the top of it and his horse has left an imprint as proof.

The stone is reasonably clean as big rocks go but it crosses my mind that someone must maintain it. I imagine an Arab employee from Heathrow airport, casually hunchbacked and shuffling across it with a dustpan and long stick and a brush, flicking up the fag ends of tourists from its hallowed surface whilst people kneel beneath in the cave of prayer.

The light is going as we leave and replace our shoes and a creamy orange light bathes the contours of the rooftops before dying quite suddenly.

Wednesday November 23. A long, long day.

A 6 am start out into a morning of perfect serenity. The low sunlight catches the windows as we drive off, sending out signals of gold along the plunging skylines which mask the hilly region Jerusalem is built upon. The city is sleepy still and everywhere we catch sight of the light at play.

The desert glows like gigantic mounds of spices left to dry in the sun. Army tents obtrude on tonal bands of subdued colour.

Ragged lump of material, a beggar, stooped almost into a ball, holds out a cranelike arm as though the limb is in a permanent position, set solid in cement.

Jericho, oldest city and scene of some of the most extraordinary archaeological finds. I ferret around and discover a torch battery, a Coke bottle and a fag end of unknown vintage.

Kibbutzim along the Jordan West Bank right up to the border fence. Breeze block huts for demobbed army personnel. Arab settlements in pathetic disarray but interspersed with impressive well ordered crops developed from the determined farming techniques of the Israelis.

Tiberius, hot springs, Sea of Galilee sublime blue, calm magical. Pilgrims from Missouri touch the Jordan and bow in prayer.

Up towards the northern end of the Golan Heights, overlooking the Hula Valley from the Syrian side.

Before the Yom Kippur War of 1973 the Syrians honeycombed the mountain top with miles of trenches. They are built from the dark volcanic rocks of surrounding areas and look like rows of rotting teeth. From this vantage point, one of the most important and threatening three kilometres on Israel's borders, the Syrians for twenty years made sitting ducks of the Kibbutz dwellers in the valley below.

A road of fine sand runs parallel to the border barrier which is patrolled daily by armoured trucks pulling large rakes. This is intended to be a foolproof method of showing whether anyone has tried to cross

New Refugee Camp - Gaza.   Ralph STEADman 74

the border illegally, as the road itself is too wide for the average Olympic jumper. The bird on the fence is a bulbul, common to the West Bank.

My preconceptions of Kibbutz life are shaky when we arrive at Kfar Hamass. Freed of the pressures of everyday worries like tax problems, bills, rat racing, I find the Kibbutz dwellers are able to enjoy to the full the simple ethic that work is good but no man shall profit by another's labour; money earned is directed to the common good.

A community spirit runs through all the activities. The dwellings, solid and adequate, are provided. Heat, light and any other necessities are provided. The land on which their settlements are situated is leased to them by the National Fund. The foundation fund of the Kibbutz itself provides the money for building and development. Children have their own houses and so both parents work a full day, happy in the knowledge of their offspring's well being.

Artists, writers and musicians are not discouraged, but must work a rota system of six weeks at a bench or in the fields, even in the kitchen, and then they can indulge themselves for the next six weeks if lucky enough to feel inspired at that particular time.

Thursday. A day on the Gaza Strip can be a romp on the sand dunes, a swim in the sea or a tour of refugee camps.

A refugee in the dictionary is a person who becomes stateless and who seeks. In reality, a refugee is also a pawn, a burden and a private world of emotional wreckage.

I am to meet an Israeli army officer for the first time. Shagra, for that is his name, is to be my guide and fulfil a request to see a refugee camp or even two.

We sit drinking coffee for nearly an hour whilst he curtly tells me all I should know before showing me around. To him the solution to a complex problem is standardisation. Even tents in rows like terraced houses would be a solution. He firmly believes he is in the right – organising people, rehousing them in what to him is perfectly acceptable accommodation, but devoid of any individual imprint. It's typical of group governmental thinking, no matter how well meaning. How does a regimented mind appreciate the colourful idiosyncrasies of an itinerant race of people?

Shagra is most anxious to show me first the local industries of the Gaza Strip, subsidised by the Israeli military government, providing work for the indigenous population and refugees specifically. No outsiders are offered employment. The only people from outside who are employed are the bosses.

A Frenchman from Marseilles, now an Israeli, runs an excellent line in Louis XV reproduction furniture which isn't quite what I expected to find. Machine tools are turning. Metalwork is very much on an industrial scale. No ethnic local industries – hard core utility.

At the refugee camp. New – no better or worse than any council estate anywhere in England, though it's warmer. One-eighth of an acre is offered to an Arab family to build their own house on or they

215

Early morning on the Front, Tel Aviv — ancient men keep their old young bodies in trim. Weathered, sun bronzed, wrinkled and fit. They keep pace + puff in all directions. Ralph STEADMAN 78

ean buy it complete – an adequate prefab.

Israel wants to exist. To feel secure they must continue to push. The Arabs resent the push and retaliate. Both big powers try in their own way to express their views but these are misconstrued by Arab and Israeli suspicion. Jealous lovers! Both need US and even Russian interest. Both distrust it. The PLO say their rights are NOT NEGOTIABLE. So are everyone's. The difficulties stem from neither side realising and accepting this fact.

Here he comes! Sadat. The faces of delight – soldiers, guards. I didn't want them to go to all this trouble. The shalom service lady walks towards me. This is it. I straighten up and try to look sober.

'Mr Steadman?'

'Yesh, thash me, sweetheart. Where d'ya put thosh Jewish welcome drinksh?'

'Er, Mr Steadman – Mrs Simulian regrets she cannot meet you. They've annexed the Sinai desert for the visit of Mr Sadat and raised the Dead Sea. She's somewhere in the middle of it on her way here. Jerusalem is under siege and the Red Sea has been parted, miracles are being performed, but do you think you can make your own way? Are you all right? Mr Steadman? You look quite pale. Here, let me lend you this *What's on in Tel Aviv* – you can give it me back some other time.'

State of the Nation

Stumblebum for President

'Vote for me, buddy, this is a tough city to get started in.'

The croaking voice came from somewhere dark, foul and salivary on my immediate left. Something gripped at my arm and I turned my head wildly as my right hand reached instinctively in my pocket for a quarter – as it does on Skid Row.

The head from whence the voice came shook slowly. 'No, buddy, I want your vote this time. I'll take your money when I'm President.'

'Uh? What? Yeah? Too much bad hooch,' I thought to myself, catching sight of the bottle as I scanned the shape clinging to my left arm like a praying mantis and pressing its head forward earnestly.

'Of course, my friend,' I replied trying to remain aloof whilst I humoured this wretch. Our eyes met. Two awesome hollow caverns on either side of its blue beaten nose opened up, bloodshot and raw. 'Been a long campaign, eh?'

'Yup.'

' – and November 3rd already,' I continued. 'Election Eve.'

The figure stumbled backwards and managed a precarious balance with the help of my left arm. He lifted an uncertain finger and tried to point it at me.

'Hey – are you English?'

'Well, Welsh actually,' I replied. 'Does it show?'

'Naw, but you can be my Foreign Policy Adviser.'

'Er, yes, of course. Anything you say. Now I really must be on my

way. I have an important interview on AVAO – WC OPTV to publicise my new book, *God was on His Side: A Story of Thwarted Impeachment.*'

'Hell, man! I'll come with ya. You can be my Press Secretary!'

'Now look,' I said wrenching my arm free from his bony grip. 'This is getting out of hand and I'll be late. Take a dollar instead,' and I thrust a note down the front of his grime-shiny service overcoat.

'Nope! Bribery won't work, buddy – not in my administration, and anyway, until I get my hands on some tax legislation, it's only worth sixty-seven cents. I'm gonna reduce federal spending to cut taxes and I'll reflate the economy with a stronger defence budget.'

'Holy shit!' I replied, horrified. 'You sound like Ronald Reagan!'

'Goddamn, I *am* Ronald Reagan!!!' and the swaying creature took a swig from its cracked bottle. It was a horrible sight and I backed off staring in disbelief at the stricken figure before me. It wasn't possible, and yet – that matted black hair, that strong hairline sloping down the weather-wrinkled forehead on its left side. The mouth, such as it was, a twisted upper lip tightening to reveal broken uneven premolars, aided by a tongue poking through to prevent the bottom lip quivering uncontrollably to join again with its partner, as the head leered in an attempt to smile. It was sickly.

The creature sensed the shock of recognition flitting across my delicate Celtic features flushed with early morning dyspepsia. I looked about me half wanting to escape. A filthy once-white stetson lay crumpled in a doorway like a sleeping drunk amidst broken bottles, cigarette packets, half eaten hamburger buns and human excreta.

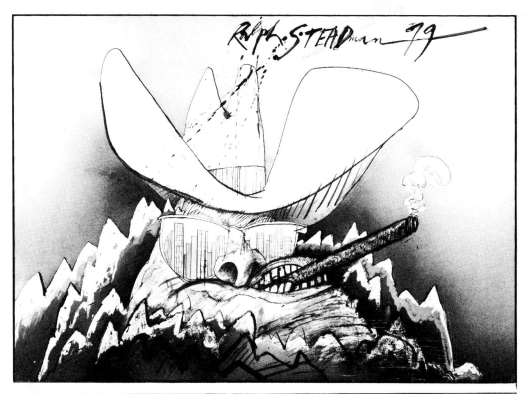

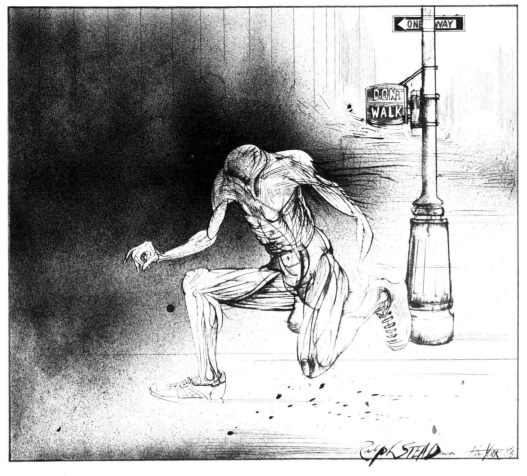

Limp figures rolled and lurched in slow motion in the middle of a road scarred with potholes and junk. Stores and warehouses appliquéd with rusty iron shutters and fading shop signs lined the street like rotting teeth against the Wall Street skyline.

'See that one?' wheezed the creature, coughing up a gob of dark red spittle on to the crumbling sidewalk and pointing to a figure spreadeagled against a sea of tiny bricks which could be straight out of a Ben Shahn painting of city life.

Wearing only a long black cassock over Superman shorts and a T shirt with a big C emblazoned across the chest, the figure held its arms high and flat against the brickwork, an empty bottle labelled POWER in one hand and a Bible in the other. A mission bell black hat sat hard down over a broken rubber face.

'Throw them! Throw them!!' it moaned. 'Throw your stones. I don't care. I can take it. I can take it all, but don't – please don't – reject me!' This pathetic vision of shattered hopes slid down the wall and sank to its knees convulsed in deep sobs.

It got up again.

'Be guided by a sense of long range commitment to peace, be you black or white, Jew or Christian, friend or foe. All are welcome. Hot soup for all!'

The figure sank again weeping hideously.

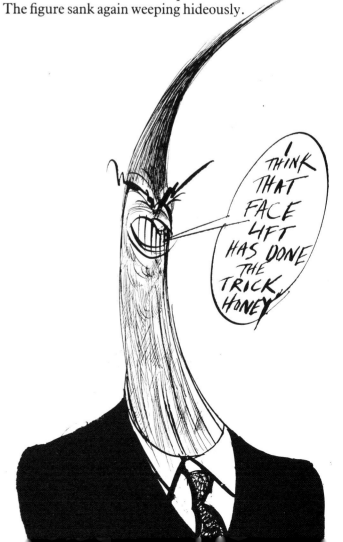

'Come back, come back,' it said. 'I forgive you – having no foreign policy is not the end of the world. I too am a hostage in my own land. I forgive yoooooooo! Four more years, please. I beg you. Show compassion. Compassion is man's only way to acknowledge human frailty with honour. The President is not an empty carcass!'

At this point the figure threw up amongst the broken glass. It continued, 'He's flesh and blood like you. Please help me. I am a stranger in a strange land – a moving living thing in a rigid frame. Give me air – give me air! I cannot breathe in iron.'

The figure twitched, cast glazed eyes around itself, saw nothing and slumped across a broken window frame, motionless.

'Holy mother of God!' The words fell from my lips like wet confetti. 'It's him. It's Jimmy Carter. Isn't it? It can't be!'

'It is, my friend. Punch drunk in adversity. Not even cheap hooch did that. He doesn't even belong here. In that respect, he's a phoney!'

'It's horrible – '

'It's life and it's not him you see up there on the hustings, in the oval office, getting out of a helicopter, shaking hands. That's only a Muppet.'

An aimless soul draped in sartorial disrepair wandered zig zag between us, wandered on, and disappeared into the dark doorway of a bankrupt jeweller's shop.

'Was that Jody Powell – or Pat Buchanan?'

I stared at the nightmare in the service overcoat at my side and it leered back at me to dispel any possible doubt.

'A Muppet?' I enquired.

'Either,' it replied and shuffled forward to grip my right arm this time. Bloodshot yellowed balls in sockets looked up at me seductively. I was seduced.

'C'mon,' said the mouth beneath them. 'Let's get down to the TV station. They'll believe you. You have honest eyes.'

221

I took another look at the roaming, lurching, slow motion figures falling on their faces. The Strausses, the Jordans and Petersons. I felt warm inside, horribly warm.

A checker cab pulled up.

'Wanna cab, sir?' asked the driver.

'No thanks,' I said, 'I'm just going round the corner.'

'OK, suit yourself,' and the cab drove off and disappeared.

I put a protective arm over the hunched shoulders of the creature with the cracked half-empty bottle and I leaned to its lurching path. I felt its hand grip my shoulder in comradely fashion. Opening my eyes I lifted my head slowly from the beer-soaked table as the barman shook me.

'C'mon, buddy. Time to move on. I'm closin' up.'

'Ah yes, sorry. Must have been that last drink. Been a busy day.'

'Sure, pal. Goodnight.'

I made my way towards the curtained doorway at the end of the bar and a thought struck me.

'Funny,' I said, and the barman looked up as he turned the last chair on to a table.

'I was just thinking – that's the first time a taxi ever stopped in New York and asked if I wanted a lift.'

The barman looked puzzled, sniffed then answered me. 'Taxis *never* stop, sunshine, unless you hail them. You musta been dreamin'.'

I walked out on to the pavement of a quiet street, 56th I think, between 5th and 6th, turned up my collar and set off for the hotel. There were no taxis at this time of night. The steam from the sewer grids rose up white like hungry ghosts. A dark figure stumbled out of the shadows and gripped me by the left arm. 'Give us a dime, buddy. This is a tough city to get started in.' He looked like no one I knew. His hair sat thick and pure white on his head like a halo. His fine boyish features . . .

223

Gardening Hint No. 12

Eureka Stockade was the name of a film made in 1947. A spectacular drama of Australia's gold rush. It starred Chips Rafferty and Jane Barrett with Jack Lambert and Gordon Jackson in supporting roles, all chosen for their ability to do a passable imitation of an Australian accent. A rare gift at that time, though I might mention at this delicate juncture that Reginald Bosanquet, England's answer to John Chancellor, is pretty good at it now in 1974.

I must have been a mere forty-two at the time; my first drawing was still burning behind my eyes, bringing tiny beads of sweat to my smooth marble forehead. I sat transfixed before this saga, third row from the back, popcorn in one hand, my mother in the other. The English Army (Ninth Heavy Fusiliers, or 'Colony Crushers' as they were known) was about to quell the madness often brought on when some damn fool shouts 'Gold!' Amidst the scramble of film extras and walk-on parts, my fast-developing powers of observation noticed a minute blue flower crushed beneath the wheel of a six and seven-eighths of an inch calibre Hearst and Palliser field cannon.

It was the one detail in the whole film that jarred and made me shudder. It was a Primula Obconica, and I know for a fact that when crushed, this flower gives off an intensely strong and beautiful fragrance that promotes a craving to love your fellow men, brings peace to the soul and finally skin rash.

So why were these guys fighting? That's what I want to know. Any old excuse for violence, that's what I say.

However, I can't change the world or silly film directors, but I can make the ideal indoor compost heap with a dozen or so of these plucky little flowers based on the theory of

opposing smell cancellation by Dr Marcus Krettner. Merely crush their tiny stalks with a steak hammer and, a peg on your nose, place them at the bottom of any tinned food carton or tea chest, cover with an old-style Rolling Stone *journal and you have formed the foundation of a compost heap you can keep under the kitchen sink. It's the only genuine recycling waste disposal unit I know. Just throw it all in there and a rich fertile humus will be yours as time goes by and love grows old.*

Next time: 'Plant a Tree in Times Square Revolution' Year.

225

DE-FILED

From secrecy and deceit
Come back America
From South East Asia and
    Vietnam
Come back America
This is also a time not for death
    but life.
20,000 have come home in 1968
And one whose heart has ached
    for ten years.
There will be no more talk.
Never again will we send young
    blood to prop up a corrupt
    military government abroad.
Come home America.

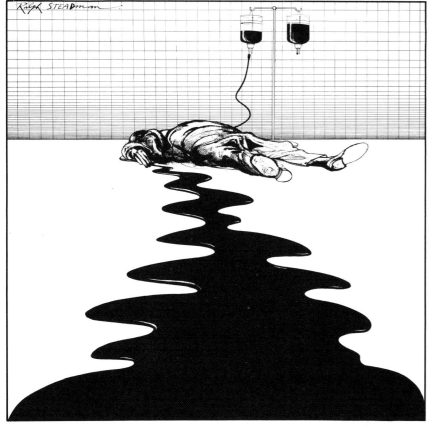

The Falklands G.C.E. exam question: If it takes 5,000 troops 14 weeks to move 2,000 Argentines in 5 ships back to Buenos Aires, how long would it take Mrs Thatcher on her own?

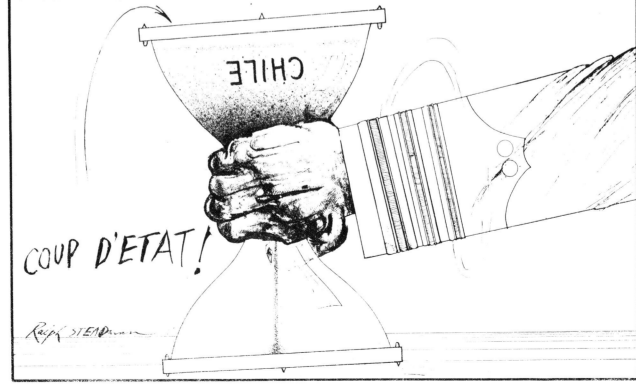

The Artists' MOTHER

…AND HIS MODEL-IN-LAW

Every real artist has a model. Rubens had dozens of them. Great pendulous pink
women with mountains of flesh. It's no good copying his. You have to get your own.
I became acquainted with my model when she rang to ask if I wouldn't mind doing
her a drawing in aid of the release of a Russian dissident writer. He was ultimately
released and Pamela Manson, for that is her name, a Brighton actress who is so
talented she can perform on both sides of the stage at once, is eternally grateful. As
far as she's concerned I'm a wonderful chap who can do no wrong.
    I had found my model at last and she agreed to pose for me as long as my
mother-in-law was present. So that's how it was, but only for photographs because
she gets cold hanging about and so does my mother-in-law.
To her eternal credit, Pamela is a natural in front of the camera, a real trooper whose
endowments turn photography into a joyous romp. This is my tribute to her – and to
my mother-in-law, Ruby.

Upset her for as little as £3.

JOIN THE LABOUR PARTY.

My sister and her granddaughter.

TORIES

Tory is the name given to a political party but it is of uncertain origin. It is generally believed to be Irish, possibly derived from the word 'toree' which means 'give me'. It was used as a noun to name a robber. There is also another Irish word it was used in connection with, 'tornigh' – to pursue.

Daniel Defoe claims it was used during Queen Elizabeth's reign to categorise the Irish rebels and he represented the Irish as robbers who preyed upon the country.

The word 'tory' first entered English politics in 1679 when a bill was introduced to exclude the Duke of York from the succession. The opposition to the Bill were called Tories and from that moment Tories became the court party. Their unshakeable belief in passive obedience and the divine right of kings sanctified by the Church of England became their hallmark.

Their opponents, the Whigs, derived their strange name from a drink swigged by Scotsmen fighting for their rights and religious beliefs. The drink anaesthetised these stalwart people against the vile onslaught of an English government of Tories who did not believe they had any.

Political drawing is the only kind of art that is not merely decorative and that makes it a very honourable pursuit.

It appears to manifest itself in its purest and best form only when the need is greatest and that makes it heroic. In the finest examples of this art form, only the very essence of a subject's message is portrayed. All extraneous matter is left out in the interests of clarity and the urgent need to communicate a powerful thought in the name of some cause or other, be it right or wrong.

When the picture, portrait or cartoon is meant to extol the virtues of national idealism and warlike tendencies, or when it describes harrowing plight of groups of people, or when it forms an attack against a dictator or scurrilous tyrant, the best images are still the simplest, the most urgent and ultimately the most necessary.

The driving force is common to all such images whatever the artists' beliefs or cultural backgrounds. The common bond, whatever the message, is the urge to convey a statement as powerfully as possible in an attempt to short-circuit time and tell all in an instant.

The more urgent the message, and the more committed the artist to a cause, the more potent is the result. Once seen by the viewer, the image has served its purpose and is then virtually worthless. This is largely true, except that many artists have burned with a passion transcending the cause and so the work has found another level of aesthetic power and value in its own right.

The cause is usually one of common humanity and universal values and so the work is not affected by the passage of time unless its power and authority are increased with hindsight.

231

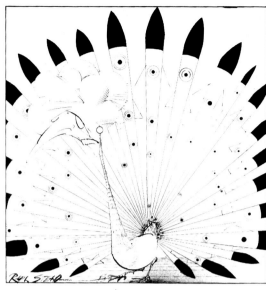

The unique power of politically motivated images is at its weakest when the artists have exercised their talents through the good offices of the state which has hired them (usually in wartime), to promote the virtues of national pride. The artists are lost within a cause beyond their ken. The images are wooden and puerile, devoid of wit or humour and serve only to demonstrate with clarity a sworn affidavit to a fatuous lie signed by the state. A barefaced, blind and patent immorality: might is right and therefore we should all go forward together in the name of national morale.

Nothing has demonstrated that ever-present tendency in nations more than the climate prevailing and expressed through our media coverage during the Falklands crisis in 1982.

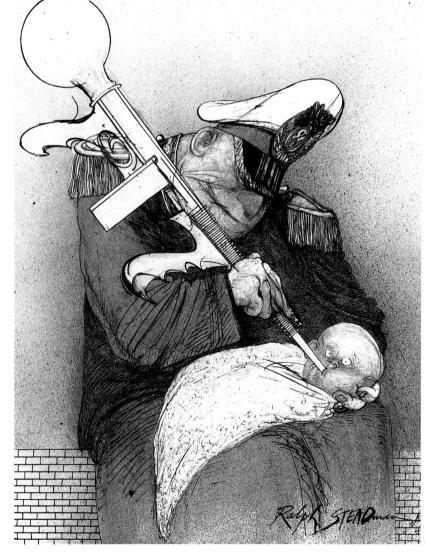

233

MAGGIE & CHILD - CHRISTMAS 1983

THE TUNNEL AT THE END OF THE LIGHT

ARTIST'S NOTE: IF I'VE HEARD IT ONCE
I'VE HEARD IT A HUNDRED TIMES —
"GEE! THAT IRON LADY OF YOURS IS
SOME WOMAN — PUTTIN' YOUR COUNTRY BACK
IN SHAPE AND STUFF LIKE THAT.
GIVIN' THE LITTLE MAN A BREAK
SHOWIN' THEM UNION GUYS WHERE TO
GET OFF — KINDA LIKE WORLD
WAR II, HUH?

THE SUPPOSITION PEGGED
THE DRAWING!!

THE BRINK

7ᵖ

Pity. She was a game old bird.
Never thought she'd do *that* – *and* get
found out. Don't make 'em like her
any more. Still, she couldn't have
carried on – not for much longer
anyway – without it noticing.

234

Leonardo and Me

I, Leonardo: December 16, 1982. Today Anna opened her little nursery school, and the idea of how I should approach the book occurred to me: I would write it in the first person. I would look through his eyes. Then I would know what it really felt like – no experts can tell me. This allowed me complete artistic licence and afforded me the luxury of telling 'my' life story without the doubts that accompany biographies.

Photograph by Susan Gray. Figure by Lyn Kramer.

The Flying YoYo. 22 Nov. 83

235

'Theatre is for the bored, the disenchanted, the hangers-on, the dreamless, the frustrated – and anyone else who doesn't know how to entertain themselves.' (Who said that? circa 1980.) My own musical, *I, Leonardo*, is only just emerging. Emerging as only a masterpiece can, painfully but inevitably. If it is giving me pleasure and pain in equal measure, you can be sure others will love it too.

We live in a time when the world needs a powerful injection of hope and personal achievement. Nothing cynical will serve our purpose now. Nothing smart-arsed or gross will do. It must seem real, weird and extraordinary, but within our reach.

Unfortunately, behind the most inspiring of theatrical extravaganzas seethe the oily dark waters of management – the

ooze of percentage. I hesitate to put a foot in, and two are out of the question. From Denmark Street to Broadway these waters swirl and heave with suckfish feeding off the struggling victims of showbiz razzmatazz. Shoals of parasites emerge from the mud on the bottom and sink tiny hookteeth into flesh and the body dies along with the inspiration. No place for an innocent like me, unless I go down in a diving bell, which is what Leonardo would have done.

To ensure the purity of my involvement and influence over such events certain precautions must be taken or the game is lost before it's even begun.

I always ask the same question when confronted with a dilemma: 'What would Leonardo have done?' Regarding his musical, and it is his, because it is mine, he said get it right. So I will.

237

Photograph by kind permission of Philip Sayer.

Bibliography

Unless otherwise stated, all works listed were published in London.

I Books by Ralph Steadman

Ralph Steadman's Jelly Book, Dobson Books, 1967.

The Little Red Computer, Dobson Books, 1968.

The Yellow Flowers, Dobson Books, 1968.

Still Life with Raspberry or The Bumper Book of Steadman, Rapp and Whiting, 1969.

Dogsbodies, Abelard-Schuman, 1970; Paddington Press, revised edition, 1977. As *A Leg in the Wind and Other Canine Curses*, Arrow Books (Hutchinson), 1982. As *No Good Dogs*, Putnam, New York, 1983.

Ralph Steadman's Bumper to Bumper Book for Children, Abelard-Schuman, 1972; Pan, 1973.

America, Straight Arrow, New York, 1974.

The Bridge, William Collins, 1974.

Flowers for the Moon, Nord Sud Verlag, Zurich, 1974; Andersen Press, revised edition, 1983.

Sigmund Freud, Paddington Press, 1979; Aubier, Paris, 1980; Wouter Wagner B.V., Amsterdam, 1980; Rowolht, Hamburg, 1981; Penguin, 1982.

The Curse of Lono (with Hunter S. Thompson), Bantam Books, New York, 1983; Pan Picador, 1984.

I, Leonardo, Jonathan Cape, 1983; Aubier, Paris, 1983; Summit Books, New York, 1983.

II Books illustrated by Ralph Steadman

This is Television by Richard Carrickford, Frederick Muller, 1958.

Private Eye's Romantic England, Weidenfeld and Nicolson, 1963.

Das Eichhorn und Das Nashornchen by Mischa Damjan, Nord Sud Verlag, Zurich, 1964. As *The Big Squirrel and Little Rhinoceros*, Norton, New York, 1965.

Fly Away Peter by Frank Dickens, Dobson Books, 1964; new edition, 1967.

Love and Marriage by Daisy and Angela Ashford, Rupert Hart-Davis, 1965; new edition, OUP paperback, 1982.

The Penguin Private Eye, Penguin, 1965.

Book of Boobs, Private Eye Productions Ltd, 1966; André Deutsch, 1973.

Where Love Lies Deepest by Daisy Ashford, Rupert Hart-Davis, 1966.

Alice in Wonderland by Lewis Carroll, Dobson Books, 1967 (Winner of the Francis Williams Book Illustration Award 1972).

Die Falschen Flamingos by Mischa Damjan, Nord Sud Verlag, Zurich, 1967. As *The False Flamingoes*, Dobson Books, 1968.

The Thoughts of Chairman Harold, compiled by Tariq Ali, Gnome Press, 1967.

The Little Prince and the Tiger Cat by Mischa Damjan, McGraw-Hill, New York, 1968.

Private Eyewash, Macdonald, 1968.

The Tale of Driver Grope by Richard Ingrams, Dobson Books, 1969.

Born under a Bad Sign by Tony Palmer, William Kimber, 1970.

Timothy Winters by Charles Causley, Contemporary Poets Set to Music Series, No. 7, Turret Books, 1970.

Two Cats in America by Mischa Damjan, Longman Young Books, 1970.

Fear and Loathing in Las Vegas: a savage journey to the heart of the American Dream by Hunter S. Thompson, Straight Arrow, New York, 1971; Granada Paladin, 1972.

150 Careers in Advertising by Patricia Mann, Longman, 1971.

Alice Through the Looking Glass by Lewis Carroll, MacGibbon and Kee, 1972.

Night Edge, poems by Jane Deverson, Bettiscombe Press, 1972.

Der Schlafhund und der Wachhund by Kurt Baumann, Nord Sud Verlag, Zurich, 1972. As *Daisy and Hawkeye*, Hutchinson, 1974.

Two Poems of Night by Edward Lucie-Smith, Turret Books, 1972.

Image Reality and Superreality by Edward Lucie-Smith, 1972-3.

Fear and Loathing on the Campaign Trail by Hunter S. Thompson, Straight Arrow, 1973; Allison & Busby, 1974.

A Little Treasury of Limericks Fair and Foul by John Letts, André Deutsch, 1973.

The Rabbit, poem by Edward Lucie-Smith, Turret Books, 1973.

The Hunting of the Snark by Lewis Carroll, Michael Dempsey in association with Studio Vista, 1975.

The Poor Mouth by Flann O'Brien, Hart-Davis, MacGibbon, 1975.

Cherrywood Cannon, story by Dimitri Sidjanski, Paddington Press, 1978.

Emergency Mouse by Bernard Stone, Andersen Press, 1978; Sparrow Books paperback edition, 1981. As *Souris en blanc*, Les Editions de La Murelle, 1979, and Editions Gallimard, 1980. Also translated into Dutch, German, Italian, Japanese and Swedish.

Inspector Mouse by Ralph Steadman and Bernard Stone, Andersen Press, 1980; Sparrow Books paperback edition, 1982. As *Touchez pas au Roquefort*, Editions Gallimard, 1980. Free Spirit Productions, Amsterdam, 1983 (Winner of the Silver Brush Award).

A Note on Mice, poem by Edward Lucie-Smith, Turret Books, 1981.

For Beauty Douglas: Adrian Mitchell's Collected Poems 1953-79, Allison & Busby, 1982.

Quasimodo Mouse by Ralph Steadman and Bernard Stone, Andersen Press, 1984.

III Periodical and book contributions by, interviews with and articles on Ralph Steadman

Abergele Visitor, 'Awards for Abergele Cartoonist', Abergele, June 17, 1977.

Ambiente, article and photo essay by Peter Hays and Peter Moody, Meyer, Hamburg, March 1982.

Ambit, illustrations.

Aquarius, illustrations.

The Art of Caricature by Edward Lucie-Smith, Orbis, 1981.

Bent, 'Steadman's Popes', No. 1.

Blitz, interview by Johnny Black, Dec. 1983/ Jan. 1984.

Book Fair brochure for Abelard-Schuman, 8 cartoons, 1973.

Books and Bookmen, 'Through the Looking Glass', May 1974.

La Caricature: art et manifeste, Ronald Searle/ Roy/Bornemann, Skira, Geneva, 1974.

Covent Garden Carrot, drawings and story with Bernard Stone, Nos 1 & 2.

Creative Review, article by Jennifer Manton, May 1983.

Daily Mail, Beer Mats, Feb. 11, 1980.

Daily Telegraph Magazine, 1984 drawings, No. 515, Sept. 20, 1974.

Design and Art Direction, Leonardo article by Beryl McAlhone, Nov. 1983.

The Diary, edited and published by Robert Pollock, fashion cartoons, 1968.

Eastword, the Eastern Arts Association, article.

Fiction, 'Flann O'Brien', Vol. 3, No. 1, New York.

Graphics World, article by Mandie Rickaby on illustrations for children, No. 36, May/ June 1982.

Graphis, article on *I, Leonardo* by Stanley Mason, No. 208, Zurich, 1984.

Guardian, review of *Freud* drawings by Michael McNay, July 6, 1982.

Hullfire student magazine, interview by Roger Everatt, Hull, April 28, 1977.

Illustrators, article by Rufus Segar, No. 30, 1980.

The Indignant Years, edited by H.E. Salisbury and D. Schneiderman, Crown Publishers/ Arno Press, New York, 1971.

Liverpool Echo, interview by Derrick Hill, Liverpool, Oct. 22, 1973.

Man Bites Man, edited by Steven Heller, A & W Publishers, New York, 1981.

New Departures, article, No. 15, 1983.

New Review, article, Vol. 3, No. 36, March 1977.

New Society, article by Peter Fuller, Jan. 1, 1976.

New Statesman, cartoons, 1978-.

New York Times Magazine, 'Leonardo à la Steadman' by Sherwin D. Smith, New York, Oct. 9, 1983.

Opus International, cartoons, Nos 31/32, Paris, 1972.

Preuves, 'L'oppression vue par Ralph Steadman', No. 18, Paris, 1974.

The Prickly Muse by Hans Hubmann, Bruckmann Munchen, Munich, 1974.

Private Eye, cartoons, 1960s.

Punch, cartoons, 1960s.

Rocky Mountain Magazine, article by Steven Heller, Nov. 1979.

Rolling Stone Magazine, cartoons, New York and San Francisco, 1970s and 1980s.

Shut Up! Cartoons for Amnesty, Amnesty International, Verlag Gerhard Stalling, Hamburg, 1977. As *Ta Gueule!*, Albin Michel, Paris, 1977.

Smokestack El Ropo's Bedside Reader, excerpts from *Fear and Loathing in Las Vegas* with drawings, Straight Arrow, San Francisco, 1972.

Sunday Times Magazine, 'My Life as Leonardo', Nov. 6, 1983.

Target: The Political Cartoon Quarterly, New York, spring 1980.

Telegraph Sunday Magazine, article on *Alice in Wonderland*, autumn 1967; body painting article by Miles Kington, autumn 1969; article on *Alice Through the Looking Glass*, No. 418, Nov. 3, 1972; 'Israel', drawings, May 14, 1978; *Sigmund Freud*, review, Sept. 23, 1979; 'Skiing', drawings, Dec. 2, 1979.

Time Out, Oct. 27-Nov. 2, 1978; Jan. 29-Feb. 4, 1982; May 7-13, 1982.

T.R. (magazine in Arabic and English), cover drawings, 1976-79.

View, interview with Robert Ray, No. 2, spring/summer 1979.

Village Voice, article on Hunter Thompson and R.S. in London after Zaire by Jon Bradshaw, New York, May 19, 1975.

Viz, article by Ferry Zayadi with drawings, No. 5, 1979.

American *Vogue*, photomontage based on Snowdon pictures of R.S., New York, 1967.

Washington Post, article by Tom Zito, Washington, Oct. 8, 1972.

WLO Newspaper spread by John Spearman, April 28, 1977.

Zoom, article with drawings, No. 25, Paris, June/July 1974.

IV Portfolios

'Alice', set of 4 etchings, Editions Alecto, 1973.

'Snark', set of 6 etchings, Cassell & Collier Macmillan, 1975.

'Freud', set of 7 silk screen prints, Steam Press, 1979.

Shakespeare prints for the Royal Shakespeare Company:
  King Lear, signed edition of 100, 1980.
  Macbeth, signed edition of 100, 1982.
  Henry VIII, signed edition of 100, 1983.

'Leonardo: drawing machine', signed edition of 300, Royal Festival Hall, 1983.

'Leonardo and Michelangelo', signed edition of 250, 1984.

V Poetry Broadsheets

Portfolio No. 1 (Steam Press)

1 'Haiku', 1970.
2 'A Silly Thing to Do', Jane Deverson, 1970.
3 'Descartes', Stephen Spender, 1970.
4 'No Invader', Allan Hodgkins, 1970.
5 'The Rhino', Edward Lucie-Smith, 1971.
6 'More Than I Am', Kevin Crossley-Holland, 1971.
7 'Behind His Mask', Virginia Lawson, 1971.
8 'For Talitha 1941-1971', Christopher Logue, 1971.
9 'Crow Goes Out to Play', Ted Hughes, 1972.
10 'Boys in a Pie', John Fuller, 1972.
11 'And Sometimes It Happens', Brian Patten, 1972.
12 'Throw These Away in the Morning', Adrian Henri, 1973.

Portfolio No. 2 (Steam Press)

13 'After He Mounted Her' ('Pigeons at Villa Belmonte'), Ruth Fainlight, 1974.
14 'The Grey Penitents', Lawrence Durrell, 1974.
15 'Block Maker's Black', Asa Benveniste, 1974.
16 'To Eva Descending the Stair', Sylvia Plath, 1974.
17 'Somme', Alan Sillitoe, 1974.
18 'Narcissus Redivivus', Lyman Andrews, 1974.

Portfolio No. 3 (Steam Press)

19 'Immigrant', Fleur Adcock, 1976.
20 'Go to the Bridge Railings', Bill Butler, 1976.
21 'Obsession', Jane Deverson, 1976.
22 'Leap Off the City Skyline', David Harsent, 1976.
23 'Morning Song', Adrian Henri, 1976.
24 'Tiger Dreams', Roger McGough, 1976.
25 'The Farm Hand', Douglas Mellor, 1976.

T.R. Press

Prints: translations by Abdullah al-Udhari
'An Arab Poem', Samih al-Qasim, 1982.
'A Mirror for the Twentieth Century', Adonis, 1982.
'Earth Poem', Mahmud Darwish, 1982.

VI Exhibitions

1968 Bath Gallery (Denzil Walker). The Alice drawings.
1974 The Puck Gallery, New York. American drawings.
1972 Victoria and Albert Museum. Francis Williams Book Award Show.
1977 National Theatre. The Show: retrospective.
1983 Royal Festival Hall. *I, Leonardo*, the drawings from the book.
1984 Royal Festival Hall. *Between the Eyes:* retrospective.

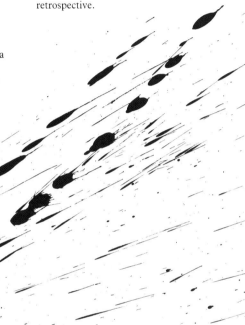

Acknowledgements

SPECIAL THANKS to many good people, many movements, many organisations and many magazines over many years. Among the magazines, I must mention the following: *Punch, Private Eye*, the *Telegraph Sunday Magazine*, the *New York Times, Rolling Stone, Esquire, Penthouse, Playboy, New Statesman, New Society, Coast, Scanlan's, Ambit, Radio Times*, the *Sunday Times*, the *Observer, Management Today, Campaign, Director, Time Out, Oui, Rocky Mountain Magazine*, the *Transmedia Letter, Le Fou Parle, Tatler, Illustrated London News, Saturday Night* (Toronto), *Weekend Magazine* (Toronto), *Radio 3, South*, the *Rebel, Running, Information Research Magazine* (Pentagram), *Knave, Oz, Running Man, Viz, J.D. Journal, Swill* and the *Progressive*.

The Gardening Notes first appeared in *Rolling Stone* during the early 1970s. I refused payment for them to keep them pure. Well, to tell you the truth nobody offered me anything, and my vanity got the better of me. I did them for love and because they were a gift to me from above, a green organism glowing on a festering wasteland. I offer them to you. Be sustained by them as I was.

These thanks and acknowledgments are rarely read, if ever, but somehow if they are not there it gets noticed, but what gets noticed more is the omission of an individual's name if the decision has been made to try to name absolutely everyone who perhaps should be mentioned, because they know one of the people who *was* mentioned and may have been involved to such an extent that they too feel that they should be mentioned.

You see the problem. The problem is starting. If you don't start, there is no problem, but you have to put something and people do genuinely want others to know if they are grateful and the prospective recipient likes to be thanked. Bless your hearts. All of you, and all of those who still might think they have been left out.